40 Days

With David

From shepherd boy To king of Israel

Mission Co-ordinator:

Dominic
Smart

BOOT CAMP

READ

LEARN

INFO

PRAY

BOOT CAMP

READ

LEARN

INFO

PRAY

Blythswood Care

CF4•K

© Dominic Smart 2008

ISBN: 978-1-84550-370-3

Published by Christian Focus Publications

Geanies House, Fearn, Tain, Ross-shire,

IV20 1TW, Scotland, UK.

www.christianfocus.com

Extra Information; Boot Camp; Words; Who's Who

© Christian Focus Publications 2008

Cover design: Alister MacInnes

Printed and bound: CPD

CF4·K
*Because you're never
too young to know Jesus*

In love a throne will be established; in faithfulness a man will sit on it – one from the house of David – one who in judging seeks justice and speeds the cause of righteousness. Isaiah 16: 5

The crowds that went ahead of him and those that followed shouted, "Hosanna to the Son of David!" "Blessed is he who comes in the name of the Lord!" "Hosanna in the highest!" Matthew 21: 9

MISSION AND TASK

Mission and Task: For the next 40 days your mission is to read through selected Scriptures from the Old and New Testaments that relate to the life of David.

READ

SCRIPTURE READINGS
Location: Pages 10–11
Description: Read through the relevant Scripture passages.

LEARN

DAILY LESSONS
Location: Pages 14–111
Description: Find out what the life of David teaches us.

EXTRA INFORMATION
Location: At different points throughout the book.
Description: Extra information.
INFO

PRAYER POINTS
Location: At the end of each reading.
Description: A time of prayer and conversation with God.
PRAY

RESEARCH FACILITY

Further information about words and concepts highlighted in the book.

WHO'S WHO

WHO'S WHO
Get introduced to the main characters on pages 114–117.

WORDS

WORDS
Root out the meanings of certain words on pages 118–125.

BOOT CAMP If you feel ready you can start the Mission by turning straight to Page 15 and getting right into the Bible. However if you feel you need some help with the basics turn to the Boot Camp section at the back of the book. This will help you to get to grips with some information before you start the main lessons.

Location: Pages 131–137

BOOT
CAMP

BOOT CAMP/001 – GETTING STARTED WITH THE OLD TESTAMENT

BOOT CAMP/002 – GETTING STARTED WITH DAVID

BOOT CAMP/003 – GETTING STARTED WITH YOU

BOOT CAMP/004 – GETTING STARTED WITH GOD

BOOT CAMP/005 – GETTING STARTED WITH JESUS CHRIST

MAPS

MAPS AND PLACE NAMES
See where it all took place on pages 126–130.

Turn the page to read
about Mission Co-ordinator
and the mission statement
from Dominic Smart.

Mission Co-ordinator: Dominic Smart.

PLACE OF BIRTH: Dominic was born in Yorkshire, but has lived in Scotland for the past twenty-seven years.

PRESENT SITUATION: He is the Minister of Gilcomston South Church in the centre of Aberdeen. He is a regular speaker at conferences and universities and is a visiting lecturer at the Highland Theological College.

FAMILY LIFE: Dominic and his wife Marjorie have three daughters and a son. They also have some pets: two cats and a Springer spaniel.

SPARE TIME: Dominic likes jazz music, films, Indian food and proper coffee but can't get enough of any of them; the nearest thing to a hobby is trying to catch up on sleep.

CHRISTIAN LIFE: He became a Christian in 1973 after an Arthur Blessitt meeting in Bradford City football ground, and for many years was involved in United Beach Missions. He has written several books, including *When We Get It Wrong*, on failure; *Grace, Faith and Glory*, on the Bible's antidotes to legalism; and *Kingdom Builders*, on Peter, Stephen and Philip in Acts.

STRANGE BUT TRUE: Dominic would like to change two things about himself – everything he does and everything he says. But even then it would probably be wrong! His only really embarrassing moment was genuinely too embarrassing to tell in public.

YOUR MISSION — SHOULD YOU CHOOSE TO ACCEPT IT ...

READ THROUGH THE LIFE OF DAVID IN 40 DAYS

It's like a Hollywood blockbuster! The life of David, the greatest king in the Old Testament, has everything that you'd want to see in an epic film. As country boy goes from nowhere to the throne of a vast empire we watch battle scenes and unexpected romance; we see huge courage, tender love, betrayal and tragedy. The hero is handsome, strong, and brave. He's the finest soldier of his day, a poet and musician and he can even dance. He's a man of deep faith with a strong will and steadfast loyalty. He can be ruthless and merciful. He makes history with his mistakes as well as his victories. He unites a nation but divides a family.

THE UNKNOWN CAMERAMAN

But what's unique about great King David is that at his best he points forward to his even greater son, King Jesus. He was born in David's line, in David's home town of Bethlehem, but he is our King for ever.

From David we learn vital lessons for our own lives about people, responsibility, leadership, purity. We see truths about God that we need to know to live well with him.

The unknown cameraman pans his lens through the years of David's life – some of them glorious and godly, others dark and dangerous. We can take David's own words to heart too. Songs that he wrote to help his people worship God have survived in the Book of Psalms. The accounts of the life and the work of Jesus, King for ever, are found in the New Testament.

Watch the epic tale unfold over the next forty days with David, with Jesus and with yourself in the picture. You can't afford to miss it, so make yourself comfortable as the titles roll, the lights go down and the movie begins.

IT BEGINS AT THE END ...

MISSION ACCEPTED?

Yes! I want to read through the life of David in the next 40 days and find out more about the truth of God and his son, Jesus Christ.

Signed:

....

Date:

....

BIBLE READINGS AND TOPICS

SECTION 1: THE END AND THE BEGINNING
Day 1 – The Closing Scene 2 Samuel 23: 1–7
Day 2 – Where it all Started 1 Samuel 16: 1–13

SECTION 2: LIVING THE REAL LIFE
David lives with God in view, which is much more realistic than those – even in Israel – who keep forgetting God.
Day 3 – Seeing Problems Truly *1 Samuel 17: 1–11 and 32–37*
Day 4 – Courage in Danger *1 Samuel 17: 38–48*
Day 5 – Faith Wins the Day *1 Samuel 17: 48–54*
Day 6 – Jesus is our Champion *Romans 7: 21–25;
        1 Corinthians 15: 51–58*
Day 7 – The Stronghold of My Life *Psalm 27*

SECTION 3: GOD'S DIFFICULT SCHOOL
David becomes a fugitive, running from jealous, mad Saul. God has vital lessons to teach him for the future in these hard times.
Day 8 – David and Saul: Beware! *1 Samuel 18: 5–15*
Day 9 – David and Saul: God First! *1 Samuel 24: 1–12*
Day 10 – David and Jonathan: Strength *1 Samuel 23: 14–18*
Day 11 – David and Ziph: Betrayal *1 Samuel 23: 14; 19–24*
Day 12 – David and Ziph: Rescue *1 Samuel 23: 24–29*
Day 13 – Jesus is our Friend *John 15: 9–15*
Day 14 – Who Rules Your Life? *Psalm 2*

SECTION 4: TO WHOM WILL YOU LISTEN?
The people that David listens to shape him well, and he avoids listening to the wrong people.
Day 15 – David and Nabal: The Fool *1 Samuel 25: 2–13*
Day 16 – David and Abigail: The Good Woman *1 Samuel 25: 14–35*
Day 17 – David and Joab: The Hater *2 Samuel 3: 17–31*
Day 18 – David and Good Men: God's Promise *2 Samuel 5: 1–5*
Day 20 – Jesus is Wise *Luke 2: 39–40; 52; Matthew 13: 52–56*
Day 21 – How will you get Near to God? *Psalm 24*

SECTION 5: GOLDEN DAYS OF GRACE
Golden Days of Grace ...in which we see promises fulfilled and David reigning well before God, despite opposition.
Day 22 – Trust God when you can Do it yourself *2 Samuel 5: 17–25*
Day 23– When God Came Home *2 Samuel 6: 17–19*
Day 24 – God's Amazing Promise *2 Samuel 7: 8–16*
Day 25 – Reflecting God *2 Samuel 9: 1–11*
Day 26 – Victory after Victory *2 Samuel 8: 1–15*
Day 27 – Jesus is the Greatest King *Revelation 19: 11*–16
Day 28 – Praise the Lord! *Revelation 19: 11–16*

SECTION 6: DARK DAYS OF SIN
These are the days in which David gives in to temptation and brings trouble upon himself and the people that he reigns over.
Day 29 – The Fatal Weakness *Deuteronomy 17: 14–17;*
       2 Samuel 11: 1–4
Day 30 – How not to Handle Temptation: Give In
       2 Samuel 11: 1–5
Day 31 – How not to Handle Sin: Cover Up *2 Samuel 11: 6–17*
Day 32 – How not to Handle Guilt: Deny It
       2 Samuel 11: 26–12: 7
Day 33 – God Wounds and Heals *2 Samuel 12: 7–24*
Day 34 – Jesus is Pure *2 Corinthians 5: 21; 1 Peter 2: 21–25*
Day 35 – What God Desires from us *Psalm 51*

SECTION 7: PAIN AND PRAISE
David's kingship seems to go from bad to worse, but God is faithful and brings it to a good end.
Day 36 – The Kingdom is Shaken *2 Samuel 15: 1–12*
Day 37 – David Flees from Danger *2 Samuel 15: 13–26*
Day 38 – Returning to Reign *2 Samuel 19: 9–23*
Day 39 – God is my Rock *2 Samuel 22: 44–23: 7*
Day 40 – Jesus is King Forever
       Isaiah 9: 6–7 and Hebrews 1: 1– 9

SECTION 1: THE END AND THE BEGINNING

DAY 1: 2 SAMUEL 23: 1-7

THE CLOSING SCENE

DAY 2: 1 SAMUEL 16: 1-13

WHERE IT ALL STARTED

BIBLE READING
2 SAMUEL 23: 1-7

These are the last words of David:

"The oracle of David son of Jesse,
the oracle of the man exalted by the Most High,
the man anointed by the God of Jacob,
Israel's singer of songs:
[2] "The Spirit of the LORD spoke through me;
his Word was on my tongue.
[3] The God of Israel spoke,
the Rock of Israel said to me:
'When one rules over men in righteousness,
when he rules in the fear of God,
[4] he is like the light of morning at sunrise
on a cloudless morning,
like the brightness after rain
that brings the grass from the earth.'
[5] "Is not my house right with God?
Has he not made with me an everlasting covenant,
arranged and secured in every part?
Will he not bring to fruition my salvation
and grant me my every desire?
[6] But evil men are all to be cast aside like thorns,
which are not gathered with the hand.
[7] Whoever touches thorns
uses a tool of iron or the shaft of a spear;
they are burned up where they lie."

Who's Who: David; Jesse
Words: Eternity; Covenant; Oracle; Salvation

Boot Camp 001/Getting started with the Old Testament
Boot Camp 002/Getting started with David
Boot Camp 005/Getting Started with Jesus Christ

THINK ABOUT IT DAY 1
WHERE IT ALL STARTED

Where is your life going? We all have dreams and ambitions: deep desires that our lives will be long and happy. But what kind of people do we want to be at the end of life?

David knows that he is right with God and that makes the closing scene a good one. Three things in particular make it good. First, it's because of God's everlasting covenant of love and God's good work that David has confidence. David has ruled well, but beneath the surface it's all been because of God. We reach a good end when we acknowledge him and give him the credit. Second, God is described as the Rock: a sure, stable and steady foundation. You can trust him when everyone else seems to abandon you. You can trust him when life seems to be falling apart; when you are falling apart. Third, there's a choice. The good end is not inevitable – it depends on how you live. You can live the evil life and if you do, you'll be cast aside for all eternity. Or you can trust in what God has done for you through Jesus and be assured of eternal security. Even though we all hope that your closing scene is a long way off, you can choose what it will be like now!

READ THIS THEN PRAY: Our hope is certain. It is something for the soul to hold on to. It is strong and secure (Hebrews 6: 19).

Prayer: Lord Jesus, the eternal security of those who trust in you was bought at a cost – your blood was shed, your life was given, you took the punishment. Teach me to realise the consequences of my sin and my need to be saved through your death on the cross. Amen.

BIBLE READING
1 SAMUEL 16: 1-13

God said to Samuel ... "Fill your horn with oil and be on your way; I am sending you to Jesse of Bethlehem. I have chosen one of his sons to be king."

² But Samuel said, "How can I go? Saul will hear about it and kill me."

The LORD said, "Take a heifer with you and say, `I have come to sacrifice to the LORD.' ³Invite Jesse to the sacrifice, and I will show you what to do. You are to anoint for me the one I indicate."

⁴ Samuel did what the LORD said. When he arrived at Bethlehem, the elders of the town trembled when they met him. They asked, "Do you come in peace?"

⁵Samuel replied, "Yes, in peace; I have come to sacrifice to the LORD. Consecrate yourselves and come to the sacrifice with me." Then he consecrated Jesse and his sons and invited them to the sacrifice.

⁶When they arrived, Samuel saw Eliab and thought, "Surely the LORD's anointed stands here before the LORD."

⁷ But the LORD said to Samuel, "Do not consider his appearance or his height, for I have rejected him. The LORD does not look at the things man looks at. Man looks at the outward appearance, but the LORD looks at the heart."

⁸Then Jesse called Abinadab and had him pass in front of Samuel. But Samuel said, "The LORD has not chosen this one either." ⁹Jesse then had Shammah pass by, but Samuel said, "Nor has the LORD chosen this one." ¹⁰Jesse had seven of his sons pass before Samuel, but Samuel said to him, "The LORD has not chosen these." ¹¹So he asked Jesse, "Are these all the sons you have?"

"There is still the youngest," Jesse answered, "but he is tending the sheep."

Samuel said, "Send for him; we will not sit down until he arrives."

¹²So he sent and had him brought in. He was ruddy, with a fine appearance and handsome features.

Then the LORD said, "Rise and anoint him; he is the one."

¹³So Samuel took the horn of oil and anointed him in the presence of his brothers, and from that day on the Spirit of the LORD came upon David in power. Samuel then went to Ramah.

THINK ABOUT IT DAY 2
THE CLOSING SCENE

The greatest king in Israel's history appears on the scene secretly and surprisingly. God rejected Saul as king because his heart was not in tune with God. He could not rule in God's way because he refused to obey God's Word. Another king, a good king, was to replace him. Bravely but hesitantly Samuel did what God said and went to Bethlehem; for David's rise to the throne started with God's will, by God's command.

Samuel discovered that appearances are no guide to true character. We are easily fooled by the image that people put on to look good. But what if someone who looks cool is actually mean and rebellious against God? What if his heart is far from God? God sees the heart and values virtue far more highly than he values outward appearances. So even though David looked good that wasn't important: God cared about what was on the inside.

God is full of surprises. David was the last person that anyone, even his Dad, would have thought of. He was the youngest son in the family and was sent away out to the fields with the sheep. But even though no one in the family thought of him, God had special work for him to do. It was by the will and the Word of God that David was chosen and anointed.

It is God who has chosen you and who has appointed you to go and bear fruit – and it will be a fruit that will last (John 15: 16). So don't worry. Even if no one else thinks you matter or that you don't look cool, your heavenly Father has a purpose for your life. He's much more interested in what's in your heart. Make sure that it's a good heart, quick to do God's will.

READ THIS THEN PRAY: Jesus said to the disciples, 'You did not choose me but I chose you and appointed you to go and bear fruit, fruit that will last' (John 15: 16).

Prayer: Lord Jesus, help me to trust you with my future for this life and the next. May I see how much I need you, always. Amen.

Who's Who: Abinadab; David; Eliab; Jesse; Samuel; Saul; Shammah
Words: Anointed; Consecrate; Sacrifice
Maps and Place Names: Bethlehem; Ramah

SECTION 2: LIVING THE REAL LIFE

DAY 3: 1 SAMUEL 17: 1-11, 32-37

SEEING PROBLEMS TRULY

DAY 4: 1 SAMUEL 17: 38-48

COURAGE IN DANGER

DAY 5: 1 SAMUEL 17: 48-54

FAITH WINS THE DAY

DAY 6: ROMANS 7: 21-25; 1 CORINTHIANS 15: 51-58

JESUS IS OUR CHAMPION

DAY 7: PSALM 27

THE STRONGHOLD OF MY LIFE

BIBLE READING
1 SAMUEL 17: 1-11; 32-37

Now the Philistines gathered their forces for war and assembled at Socoh in Judah. They pitched camp at Ephes Dammim, between Socoh and Azekah. [2]Saul and the Israelites assembled and camped in the Valley of Elah and drew up their battle line to meet the Philistines. [3]The Philistines occupied one hill and the Israelites another, with the valley between them. [4]A champion named Goliath, who was from Gath, came out of the Philistine camp. He was over nine feet tall. [5]He had a bronze helmet on his head and wore a coat of scale armour of bronze weighing five thousand shekels; [6]on his legs he wore bronze greaves, and a bronze javelin was slung on his back. [7]His spear shaft was like a weaver's rod, and its iron point weighed six hundred shekels. His shield-bearer went ahead of him. [8]Goliath stood and shouted to the ranks of Israel, "Why do you come out and line up for battle? Am I not a Philistine, and are you not the servants of Saul? Choose a man and have him come down to me. [9]If he is able to fight and kill me, we will become your subjects; but if I overcome him and kill him, you will become our subjects and serve us." [10]Then the Philistine said, "This day I defy the ranks of Israel! Give me a man and let us fight each other." [11]On hearing the Philistine's words, Saul and all the Israelites were dismayed and terrified.

[32]David said to Saul, "Let no one lose heart on account of this Philistine; your servant will go and fight him." [33]Saul replied, "You are not able to go out against this Philistine and fight him; you are only a boy, and he has been a fighting man from his youth." [34]But David said to Saul, "Your servant has been keeping his father's sheep. When a lion or a bear came and carried off a sheep from the flock, [35]I went after it, struck it and rescued the sheep from its mouth. When it turned on me, I seized it by its hair, struck it and killed it. [36]Your servant has killed both the lion and the bear; this uncircumcised Philistine will be like one of them, because he has defied the armies of the living God. [37]The LORD who delivered me from the paw of the lion and the paw of the bear will deliver me from the hand of this Philistine." Saul said to David, "Go, and the LORD be with you."

THINK ABOUT IT DAY 3
SEEING PROBLEMS TRULY

It's crucial that we learn to see life truly. The way we read the book of daily life makes all the difference to how well we live it, especially when we hit trouble.

As soon as David is chosen by God he faces a massive difficulty. In fact the difficulty has two bits to it: a massive enemy called Goliath and a massive amount of cowardice among God's people. Look at how the Israelite men see things – a great bear of a man who threatens an earthly army; but they don't see God in the valley. They know that none of them could beat Goliath in a fight so their hearts melt with fear and they run away from him.

How does David see things? He sees the whole scene truly: with God in the picture. Goliath isn't taking on an army of men, he's taking on God! David knows that God can easily help him to beat Goliath because he's seen God help him beat lions and bears already. So David offers to go out and face the giant even though David is puny by comparison. "The Lord will deliver me," he says.

It's how we see situations that counts – God is always in the valley of trouble with us. Seeing him there is the key to facing situations that could defeat us. Don't look inside yourself for strength – look to God and find your confidence in him!

READ THIS THEN PRAY: Lord, you are like a shield that keeps me safe. You help me win the battle (Psalm 18: 35).

Prayer: Lord God, sometimes life can feel overwhelming, but if I trust in you I will see things differently. You have promised to deliver me. I thank you from the bottom of my heart. Amen.

Who's Who: Goliath; Israelites; Philistines; Saul
Words: Greaves; Javelin; Shekels; Shield-bearer; Subjects; Uncircumcised
Maps and Place Names: Azekah; Ephes Dammim; Gath; Judah; Socoh; Valley of Elah

Boot Camp 004/Getting Started with God

BIBLE READING
1 SAMUEL 17: 38-48

[38]Then Saul dressed David in his own tunic. He put a coat of armour on him and a bronze helmet on his head. [39]David fastened on his sword over the tunic and tried walking around, because he was not used to them. "I cannot go in these," he said to Saul, "because I am not used to them." So he took them off. [40]Then he took his staff in his hand, chose five smooth stones from the stream, put them in the pouch of his shepherd's bag and, with his sling in his hand, approached the Philistine. [41]Meanwhile, the Philistine, with his shield-bearer in front of him, kept coming closer to David. [42]He looked David over and saw that he was only a boy, ruddy and handsome, and he despised him. [43]He said to David, "Am I a dog, that you come at me with sticks?" And the Philistine cursed David by his gods. [44]"Come here," he said, "and I'll give your flesh to the birds of the air and the beasts of the field!" [45]David said to the Philistine, "You come against me with sword and spear and javelin, but I come against you in the name of the LORD Almighty, the God of the armies of Israel, whom you have defied. [46]This day the LORD will hand you over to me, and I'll strike you down and cut off your head. Today I will give the carcasses of the Philistine army to the birds of the air and the beasts of the earth, and the whole world will know that there is a God in Israel. [47]All those gathered here will know that it is not by sword or spear that the LORD saves; for the battle is the LORD's, and he will give all of you into our hands." [48]As the Philistine moved closer to attack him, David ran quickly towards the battle line to meet him.

Who's Who: Goliath; Philistine; Saul
Words: Tunic; Sling; Staff

Boot Camp 004/Getting started with God

THINK ABOUT IT DAY 4
COURAGE IN DANGER

Look at those last few words. David ran at the enemy!

Courage isn't what we show when we don't see any dangers; courage is when we do see danger but we don't run away. David knew that Goliath was no pussy cat, but because he saw the situation truly – with God in the picture – he knew that he didn't need to flee in order to be safe. So he shows the courage that faces and runs at Goliath. The odds against David look overwhelming if you don't see God. But David does, so he is not cowardly nor stupid: he's brave.

You have to be brave in life and when you know that God is with you courage rises in your heart whenever danger rises against you. It's not that you see yourself as super-strong, it's that you know that God is super-strong. Maybe you're up against big problems today. Well, the God who helped David run towards the battle line is with you right now. God once said to another of his friends "Have I not commanded you? Be strong and courageous. Do not be terrified; do not be discouraged, for the LORD your God will be with you wherever you go" (Joshua 1: 9). He says the same to you today.

READ THIS THEN PRAY: God cares for you, so turn all your worries over to him (1 Peter 5: 7).

Prayer: Lord God, when I feel anxious remind me to give all my worries to you. When things are going well remind me to be thankful to you. May I have the wisdom and the courage to face whatever comes. You are with me - you are all I need. Amen.

BIBLE READING
1 SAMUEL 17: 48-54

[48]As the Philistine moved closer to attack him, David ran quickly towards the battle line to meet him. [49]Reaching into his bag and taking out a stone, he slung it and struck the Philistine on the forehead. The stone sank into his forehead, and he fell face down on the ground. [50]So David triumphed over the Philistine with a sling and a stone; without a sword in his hand he struck down the Philistine and killed him. [51]David ran and stood over him. He took hold of the Philistine's sword and drew it from the scabbard. After he killed him, he cut off his head with the sword. When the Philistines saw that their hero was dead, they turned and ran. [52]Then the men of Israel and Judah surged forward with a shout and pursued the Philistines to the entrance of Gath and to the gates of Ekron. Their dead were strewn along the Shaaraim road to Gath and Ekron. [53]When the Israelites returned from chasing the Philistines, they plundered their camp. [54]David took the Philistine's head and brought it to Jerusalem, and he put the Philistine's weapons in his own tent.

Words: Believe; Faith; Scabbard; Worthy
Maps and Place Names: Ekron; Gath; Israel; Jerusalem; Judah; Shaaraim Road

THINK ABOUT IT DAY 5
FAITH WINS THE DAY

What a victory! What a tremendous reversal of the troubles! Before David appeared on the battle scene, the Israelites had no champion; now they've got one. Before, Goliath shouted insults at God and his people; now Goliath will never speak again. Before, the Israelites were running away; now it's the Philistines who are running as the Israelites surge forward. Before, Goliath wielded a massive sword against God's people; now that sword has been used to cut his own head off, and all his weapons are in David's tent.

God has turned the whole thing around through the faith of one man. Victory has been snatched from the jaws of defeat and note that all God's people share the benefits.

Jesus said that tiny faith can do great things. It's because of the greatness of the God in whom we put our trust that we can turn troubles that seem too massive for us into victories that bring glory to God and benefit God's people.

What would victory look like in the battles that you face? Who else would benefit from faith winning the day in your life? Believe that the great God of David is with you to help you in the day of trouble.

READ THIS THEN PRAY: All you people of the earth, sing to the Lord. Day after day tell about how he saves us. Tell the nations about his glory. Tell all the people about the wonderful things he has done. The Lord is great. He is really worthy of praise. People should have respect for him as the greatest God of all (1 Chronicles 16:23–25).

Prayer: Lord God, as you helped David, help me today in my troubles and difficulties. Turn my life around so that one day I will be able to look back, even at my problems, and be astonished at the wonderful things you have done for me. Amen.

BIBLE READINGS
ROMANS 7: 21–25
1 CORINTHIANS 15: 51–58

ROMANS 7: 21–25

[21]So I find this law at work: When I want to do good, evil is right there with me. [22]For in my inner being I delight in God's law; [23]but I see another law at work in the members of my body, waging war against the law of my mind and making me a prisoner of the law of sin at work within my members. [24]What a wretched man I am! Who will rescue me from this body of death? [25]Thanks be to God through Jesus Christ our Lord!

1 CORINTHIANS 15: 51–58

[51]Listen, I tell you a mystery: We will not all sleep, but we will all be changed – [52]in a flash, in the twinkling of an eye, at the last trumpet. For the trumpet will sound, the dead will be raised imperishable, and we will be changed. [53]For the perishable must clothe itself with the imperishable, and the mortal with immortality. [54]When the perishable has been clothed with the imperishable, and the mortal with immortality, then the saying that is written will come true: "Death has been swallowed up in victory." [55]"Where, O death, is your victory? Where, O death, is your sting?" [56]The sting of death is sin, and the power of sin is the law. [57]But thanks be to God! He gives us the victory through our Lord Jesus Christ. [58]Therefore, my dear brothers, stand firm. Let nothing move you. Always give yourselves fully to the work of the Lord, because you know that your labour in the Lord is not in vain.

Who's Who: Paul; Satan
Words: Labour in vain; Mortal/Immortal; Perishable/Imperishable; Resurrection; Righteous; Saviour; Wretched.
Maps and Place Names: Corinth; Rome

Boot Camp 003/Getting started with you
Boot Camp 005/Getting started with Jesus Christ

Think About It Day 6
Jesus is our Champion

The battle with Goliath was a battle fought by 'Champions'. The way it worked was that one person from each army would fight on behalf of the whole of their army. If he won, they all won; if he lost, they were all down the tubes. Everyone's future rested on the shoulders of the one warrior who would represent them as their Champion. So the Generals always sent out the best fighter to be their Champion.

We face a terrible enemy – sin and Satan. Everyone is in a battle against the power of sin now and against the power of sin to keep us captive to death in the future. We can't win against this foe ourselves. Worse, we might not even want to win – we might like sin too much!

So God sent out the best warrior to be the Champion for us. As David was the Champion for God's people against Goliath, so Jesus has been our Champion against Satan, sin and death. He defeated them for us in his righteous life, his death on the cross and his glorious resurrection from the dead. That's why it's so important to trust Jesus to be your Saviour. And it's why it's vital to keep trusting him your whole life through. In the battle against sin and the battle against death, Paul knew that Jesus gave him victory. He will give it to you too if you trust him.

READ THIS THEN PRAY: Teach me how to live as you have promised. Don't let any sin be my master (Psalm 119: 133).

Prayer: Lord God, help me to realise that I too have an enemy who would take me away from you and your Word. Protect me from temptation and from the plans of Satan. Give me your strength to resist him. Amen.

BIBLE READING
PSALM 27

The LORD is my light and my salvation – whom shall I fear? The LORD is the stronghold of my life – of whom shall I be afraid?
[2]When evil men advance against me to devour my flesh, when my enemies and my foes attack me, they will stumble and fall.
[3]Though an army besiege me, my heart will not fear; though war break out against me, even then will I be confident.
[4]One thing I ask of the LORD, this is what I seek: that I may dwell in the house of the LORD all the days of my life, to gaze upon the beauty of the LORD and to seek him in his temple.
[5]For in the day of trouble he will keep me safe in his dwelling; he will hide me in the shelter of his tabernacle and set me high upon a rock.
[6]Then my head will be exalted above the enemies who surround me; at his tabernacle will I sacrifice with shouts of joy; I will sing and make music to the LORD.
[7]Hear my voice when I call, O LORD; be merciful to me and answer me.
[8]My heart says of you, "Seek his face!"
Your face, LORD, I will seek.
[9]Do not hide your face from me, do not turn your servant away in anger; you have been my helper. Do not reject me or forsake me, O God my Saviour.
[10]Though my father and mother forsake me, the LORD will receive me.
[11]Teach me your way, O LORD; lead me in a straight path because of my oppressors.
[12]Do not hand me over to the desire of my foes, for false witnesses rise up against me, breathing out violence.
[13]I am still confident of this: I will see the goodness of the LORD in the land of the living.
[14]Wait for the LORD; be strong and take heart and wait for the LORD.

THINK ABOUT IT DAY 7
THE STRONGHOLD OF MY LIFE

This psalm is a hymn for all believers to sing. It's a testimony to how God rescues us and a prayer that he will help us and guide us. It's full of encouragement to be aware of God in troubles, to have courage and to see faith win the day.

Notice something though: what David wants most is fellowship with God. The Lord isn't just a kind of Mr Fix-it to whom David turns only when there's a problem. That approach to God just uses him: it's 'cupboard love', not real love. David loves God truly. So much so that if David could have only one thing in life, it would be closeness to God in order to worship him, admire him, seek him. David desires God more than anything else. No wonder that he trusts God more than he fears his enemies: to him, God's the greatest person in the universe; certainly greater than a few foes.

If God was only going to answer one request of yours what would you ask him for?

Complete the following sentence: One thing I ask of the LORD, this is what I seek: ...

READ THIS THEN PRAY: We are receiving a kingdom that can't be shaken. So let us be thankful. Then we can worship God in a way that pleases him. We will worship him with deep respect and wonder (Hebrews 12: 28).

Prayer: Father God, teach me how to pray to you. Help me to pray in a respectful way - not just telling you about the things that I need and want. Help me to pray to you in an intimate way - sharing my heartache and longings with you as well as seeking to know you as my Heavenly Father. Amen.

Words: Besiege; False Witnesses; Forsake; House of the Lord; Sacrifice; Tabernacle; Temple

Boot Camp 004/Getting Started with God

SECTION 3: GOD'S DIFFICULT SCHOOL

DAY 8: 1SAMUEL 18: 5-15

DAVID AND SAUL: BEWARE!

DAY 9: 1SAMUEL 24: 1-12

DAVID AND SAUL: GOD FIRST!

DAY 10: 1SAMUEL 23: 14-18

DAVID AND JONATHAN: STRENGTH

DAY 11: 1SAMUEL 23: 14; 19-24

DAVID AND ZIPH: BETRAYAL

DAY 12: 1SAMUEL 23: 24-29

DAVID AND ZIPH: RESCUE

DAY 13: JOHN 15: 9-15

JESUS IS OUR FRIEND

DAY 14: PSALM 2

WHO RULES YOUR LIFE?

BIBLE READING
1 SAMUEL 18: 5-15

[5]Whatever Saul sent him to do, David did it so successfully that Saul gave him a high rank in the army. This pleased all the people, and Saul's officers as well.

[6]When the men were returning home after David had killed the Philistine, the women came out from all the towns of Israel to meet King Saul with singing and dancing, with joyful songs and with tambourines and lutes. [7]As they danced, they sang:

"Saul has slain his thousands, and David his tens of thousands."

[8]Saul was very angry; this refrain galled him. "They have credited David with tens of thousands," he thought, "but me with only thousands. What more can he get but the kingdom?" [9]And from that time on Saul kept a jealous eye on David.

[10]The next day an evil [or harmful] spirit from God came forcefully upon Saul. He was prophesying in his house, while David was playing the harp, as he usually did. Saul had a spear in his hand [11]and he hurled it, saying to himself, "I'll pin David to the wall." But David eluded him twice.

[12]Saul was afraid of David, because the LORD was with David but had left Saul. [13]So he sent David away from him and gave him command over a thousand men, and David led the troops in their campaigns. [14]In everything he did he had great success, because the LORD was with him. [15]When Saul saw how successful he was, he was afraid of him.

Who's Who: Goliath; Saul
Words: Bless; Lutes; Prophesying

Boot Camp 004/Getting started with God

THINK ABOUT IT DAY 8
SAUL – BEWARE!

Today we follow David into 'God's Difficult School'. There are many things that he must learn before he is ready to be the king over Israel and some of those lessons will be hard. Here, David has to learn to handle an untrustworthy leader.

King Saul had gained more than anyone else from David's victory over Goliath and his other conquests over the Philistines. Many were delighted with David, but Saul's heart showed an awful trait that can emerge in so-called friends: jealousy. With Saul, whose heart was not right with God, it came from being insecure before God and it was mixed with fearful rage. It nearly cost David his life.

David never lets Saul's jealousy turn him against God. He doesn't answer rage with rage and make it worse. He gets away from the situation as best he can and he carries on doing what God had gifted him to do.

Beware! Don't be surprised if some people react badly if God blesses you. Some will be glad for you; some will be jealous. Trust God, who is always with you; don't lose your temper; walk away from the anger; carry on obeying God. People can be untrustworthy. Don't be one of them.

READ THIS THEN PRAY: Don't be upset because of sinful people. Don't be jealous of those who do wrong. Like grass, they will soon dry up. Like green plants, they will soon die. Trust in the Lord and do good. Then you will live in the land and enjoy its food (Hebrews 12: 28).

Prayer: Lord God, make me into one of those people who are joyful when you bless others. May I not be envious when others prosper. When others are envious of me help me to be kind and gracious to them. Turn my heart away from anger. Help me to obey you in all things. Amen.

BIBLE READING
1 SAMUEL 24: 1–12

After Saul returned from pursuing the Philistines, he was told, "David is in the Desert of En Gedi." [2]So Saul took three thousand chosen men from all Israel and set out to look for David and his men near the Crags of the Wild Goats.

[3]He came to the sheep pens along the way; a cave was there, and Saul went in to relieve himself. David and his men were far back in the cave. [4]The men said, "This is the day the LORD spoke of when he said to you, 'I will give your enemy into your hands for you to deal with as you wish.'" Then David crept up unnoticed and cut off a corner of Saul's robe.

[5]Afterwards, David was conscience-stricken for having cut off a corner of his robe. [6]He said to his men, "The LORD forbid that I should do such a thing to my master, the LORD's anointed, or lift my hand against him; for he is the anointed of the LORD." [7]With these words David rebuked his men and did not allow them to attack Saul. And Saul left the cave and went his way.

[8]Then David went out of the cave and called out to Saul, "My lord the king!" When Saul looked behind him, David bowed down and prostrated himself with his face to the ground. [9]He said to Saul, "Why do you listen when men say, 'David is bent on harming you'? [10]This day you have seen with your own eyes how the LORD gave you into my hands in the cave. Some urged me to kill you, but I spared you; I said, 'I will not lift my hand against my master, because he is the LORD's anointed.' [11]See, my father, look at this piece of your robe in my hand! I cut off the corner of your robe but did not kill you. Now understand and recognise that I am not guilty of wrongdoing or rebellion. I have not wronged you, but you are hunting me down to take my life. [12]May the LORD judge between you and me. And may the LORD avenge the wrongs you have done to me, but my hand will not touch you."

Who's Who: Philistines; The LORD's anointed (see David)
Words: Conscience; Prostrated
Maps and Place Names: En Gedi

34

THINK ABOUT IT DAY 9
SAUL – GOD FIRST!

David is given a clear, simple choice: put God first or put yourself first.

He knows that God wants him on the throne. He also knows that Saul is in the wrong. Here is a perfect opportunity to win the terrible contest that Saul has stirred up between them. In the cave, away from the public gaze, easy pickings. But God is in the cave. In fact, God has set the whole thing up – 'David, here's Saul in your hands; now what will you do?'

Well, David fears God more than he fears losing against Saul. And David trusts God to get him to the throne more than he trusts his own craftiness. If, at this moment, David takes matters into his own hands and forgets the God who had anointed Saul as well as him, what kind of king would he become? Not God's king ruling in God's way to God's glory. Even though his men urge him to grasp the throne, David listens to the still, small voice that says 'Put God first. Now, right now.'

READ THIS THEN PRAY: Those who belong to Christ Jesus have crucified the sinful nature with its passions and desires. Since we live by the Spirit, let us keep in step with the Spirit (Galatians 5: 23–25).

Prayer: Father God, my sinful heart wants to put my sinful desires first in my life. Other people tell me that I should put myself first, but teach me to listen to your voice instead. You should be first in my life. That is the best for me. Your ways are better than my ways and your thoughts than my thoughts. May you be the No. 1 in my life, always. Amen.

STILL SMALL VOICE: This is often used to describe the inner urging we have to do good. It is sometimes called our conscience. God speaks to us in many different ways. These can be loud and dramatic or quiet and still. It is up to us whether we listen or not. To find out another story about a still small voice, or a gentle whisper read 1 Kings chapter 19.

BIBLE READING
1 SAMUEL 23: 14–18

[14]David stayed in the desert strongholds and in the hills of the Desert of Ziph. Day after day Saul searched for him, but God did not give David into his hands.

[15]While David was at Horesh in the Desert of Ziph, he learned that Saul had come out to take his life. [16]And Saul's son, Jonathan, went to David at Horesh and helped him to find strength in God. [17]"Don't be afraid," he said. "My father Saul will not lay a hand on you. You shall be king over Israel, and I will be second to you. Even my father Saul knows this." [18]The two of them made a covenant before the LORD. Then Jonathan went home, but David remained at Horesh.

SPIRITUAL BATTLES: It's not only warriors that face up to the enemy. We've got our own share of battles to fight. We can have enemies too but often our greatest struggles and battles come at us from inside our own hearts. We all have to struggle with sin; even the apostle Paul had this problem. "I know that nothing good lives in me, that is, in my sinful nature. For I have the desire to do what is good, but I cannot carry it out. For what I do is not the good I want to do; no the evil I do not want to do–this I keep on doing. Now if I do what I do not want to do, it is no longer I who do it, but it is sin living in me that does it" (Romans 7: 18–20). This is the kind of struggle that all believers have to face. So what do you do about it? The Bible is full of good advice for us. In Ephesians chapter 6 we are told to put on the full armour of God so that we can take our stand against the devil's schemes. What is the armour of God? It is the truth and power of God's Word; the good news of the gospel of Jesus Christ, his righteousness and free salvation with the gift of faith that God gives to all who believe in his Son.

36

THINK ABOUT IT DAY 10
JONATHAN – STRENGTH

Why was David able to make the right choice before God that we read about yesterday? Partly because of his friend, Jonathan.

Saul was hounding David for his life; David's own men were often fearful or rash; there were enemies and battles all the time. Jonathan, Saul's son, David's best friend, knew that David needed cheering on. So this best friend risks his own life to go behind enemy lines and put new strength into his best friend's heart.

How does he do it? He helps him to find strength in God. He points him upwards; he reminds him of the promises of God; he encourages him to stand firm on those promises: 'You shall be king over Israel.'

And then he goes home, leaving his best friend far better prepared to face the physical battles and the spiritual ones. He might be suffering as he goes through 'God's Difficult School' but David has a true, strengthening friend to keep him going.

READ THIS THEN PRAY: A friend loves at all times and a brother is born for adversity (Proverbs 17: 17).

Prayer: Father God, thank you for your strength and friendship. Thank you that you loved me so much that you were willing to send your son, Jesus Christ, to die in my place. You have shown me real friendship, Jesus, through your sufferings. Help me to trust in you for my own salvation. May I too be a friend to others - one who will help to introduce them to you. Amen.

Who's Who: Jonathan
Words: Adversity; Believe; Believers; Covenant; Gospel
Maps and Place Names: Desert of Ziph; Horesh

BIBLE READING
1 SAMUEL 23: 14; 19–24

[14]David stayed in the desert strongholds and in the hills of the Desert of Ziph. Day after day Saul searched for him, but God did not give David into his hands.

[19]The Ziphites went up to Saul at Gibeah and said, "Is not David hiding among us in the strongholds at Horesh, on the hill of Hakilah, south of Jeshimon? [20]Now, O king, come down whenever it pleases you to do so, and we will be responsible for handing him over to the king." [21]Saul replied, "The LORD bless you for your concern for me. [22]Go and make further preparation. Find out where David usually goes and who has seen him there. They tell me he is very crafty. [23]Find out about all the hiding-places he uses and come back to me with definite information. Then I will go with you; if he is in the area, I will track him down among all the clans of Judah." [24]So they set out and went to Ziph ahead of Saul.

BETRAYAL: Godly people often face difficult situations. Those who do not trust in God may live a life of hatred towards God and his people. Jesus knows what it is like to have close friends turn against you. Peter denied that he even knew Jesus – but Judas even betrayed him to the authorities for money. The Bible tells Christians that they are not to be surprised when non-Christians hate them – because they hated Jesus first of all and most of all.

Who's Who: Ziphites
Words: Faithful; Salvation; Trustworthy
Maps and Place Names: Desert of Ziph; Gibeah; Hill of Hakilah; Horesh; Jeshimon

THINK ABOUT IT DAY 11
ZIPH – BETRAYAL

The people of Ziph certainly knew how to make life difficult for David!

They could have given him refuge – a safe place to hide, some protection and caring provision. Instead they tried to get in well with Saul. They were looking after themselves and here was a perfect opportunity to get the king on their side. They were to do the same thing again two chapters later – sell David to make themselves look good.

They are a million miles away from discerning what God is doing. Instead of strengthening David in the Lord because of God's will for David – which is what Jonathan had done – they couldn't care less what God wanted. They ignored God and put themselves first and so where Jonathan had showed loyal friendship these people show careless betrayal.

Be wise. Selfish people aren't to be trusted. They'll use you, betray you and then dump you.

READ THIS THEN PRAY: He will keep you strong to the end, so that you will be blameless on the day of our Lord Jesus Christ. God who has called you into fellowship with his Son Jesus Christ our Lord is faithful (1 Corinthians 1: 8–10).

Prayer: Lord God, you are faithful and trustworthy. May you transform me from being selfish to being a true encourager of others. Help me to trust only in those people who should be trusted. Give me the wisdom to know the difference between people who love and follow you and people who don't. Most importantly, may I trust in you for my own salvation. Amen.

BIBLE READING
1 SAMUEL 23: 24–29

Now David and his men were in the Desert of Maon, in the Arabah south of Jeshimon. [25]Saul and his men began the search, and when David was told about it, he went down to the rock and stayed in the Desert of Maon. When Saul heard this, he went into the Desert of Maon in pursuit of David.

[26]Saul was going along one side of the mountain, and David and his men were on the other side, hurrying to get away from Saul. As Saul and his forces were closing in on David and his men to capture them, [27]a messenger came to Saul, saying, "Come quickly! The Philistines are raiding the land." [28]Then Saul broke off his pursuit of David and went to meet the Philistines. That is why they call this place Sela Hammahlekoth. [29]And David went up from there and lived in the strongholds of En Gedi.

RESCUE AT CALVARY: Jesus can rescue you from the troubles you face on a day to day basis but you need to be sure that he has rescued you from the dangers of sin and death. If you trust in the Lord Jesus Christ and believe in him then his bloodshed on the cross has the power to cleanse you from all sin. Without this salvation you are in great danger – for death will be eternal death. Those who trust in the Lord Jesus Christ for the forgivenss of their sins will instead experience eternal life in heaven.

Who's Who: Philistines
Maps and Place Names: Arabah; Desert of Maon; En Gedi; Jeshimon; Sela Hammahlekoth

THINK ABOUT IT DAY 12
ZIPH – RESCUE

The story-teller flies us over the terrain as if we were in a helicopter. We look down on an arid mountain range and notice two groups of soldiers, one on each side. One group, the larger of the two, is chasing the other. The smaller group think that they are escaping but, disastrously, they don't realise that instead of moving away from the larger group they are moving towards them. These two unequal armies are about to meet at the same end of the mountain range!

But wait! A lone horseman is riding fast through the dusty desert towards the larger group of the king's men. He comes up alongside the king; we look down and see them in a brief but serious meeting. Suddenly the whole of the army of the king turns right round and the king leads them quickly away. A hair's-breadth from catching and slaughtering David and his men, they ride off in the opposite direction. David slips away.

Who is in control of your life? Who looks down lovingly from above and sees what you need, even when you don't know it yourself? Who can rescue you from dangers that you cannot see coming? Jesus.

READ THIS THEN PRAY: This then is how we know that we belong to the truth, and how we set our hearts at rest in his presence whenever our hearts condemn us. For God is greater than our hearts, and he knows everything (1 John 3: 19–20).

Prayer: Father God, you see and know everything. You know my future, the good times and the bad. You know what I need even before I ask for it. You sometimes even send me help before I know that I am going to need your help. You deserve all my thanks and praise. Amen.

BIBLE READING
JOHN 15: 9-15

[9]"As the Father has loved me, so have I loved you. Now remain in my love. [10]If you obey my commands, you will remain in my love, just as I have obeyed my Father's commands and remain in his love. [11]I have told you this so that my joy may be in you and that your joy may be complete. [12]My command is this: Love each other as I have loved you. [13]Greater love has no one than this, that he lay down his life for his friends. [14]You are my friends if you do what I command. [15]I no longer call you servants, because a servant does not know his master's business. Instead, I have called you friends, for everything that I learned from my Father I have made known to you.

LOVE: Friends love each other but perhaps we need to ask what love is? People can come up with lots of different answers but there is no better answer than what the Bible gives. We read in 1 Corinthians 13:4 that love is patient and kind. It does not envy. It does not boast. It is not proud. But if we really want to know what love is we need to look at Jesus too. In 1 John 3:16 it says that this is how we know what love is: Jesus Christ laid down his life for us.

Who's Who: Father; John
Words: Forgive

Boot Camp 005/Getting Started With Jesus Christ

THINK ABOUT IT DAY 13
JESUS IS OUR FRIEND

What a miracle! Jesus calls those who obey him to be his friends. We have to take that really seriously.

Friends like doing the same things; they're always together because they enjoy each other's company; they look out for each other; they each know what the other is doing; they keep thinking about each other; they give gifts to each other. They are friends. That's what Jesus says about us if we're following his way.

What does Jesus say we've to do? To be the very best of friends to one another – as he is to us. We've to love each other as he loves us. Even though loves costs us our lives, we are to love one another – as he has loved us though it cost him the cross.

We're maybe not brilliant friends to other people; we're maybe not brilliant friends towards Jesus. But he calls us his friends. And maybe people haven't been brilliant friends to us and have let us down. But Jesus is our very best friend. He forgives us. We need to forgive our friends too.

READ THIS THEN PRAY: A man of many companions may come to ruin, but there is a friend who sticks closer than a brother (Proverbs 18: 24).
You are my friends if you do what I command (John 15: 14).

Prayer: Lord Jesus, your obedience to your Father and your love for your people brought you to the cross and to death. May my love for others be a reflection of your love for me. You are the best friend, the most unselfish friend I could ask for. You stick closer to me than my closest family member. Help me to show my friendship for you by obeying and trusting in you. Amen

BIBLE READING
PSALM 2

Why do the nations conspire and the peoples plot in vain?
2The kings of the earth take their stand and the rulers gather together against the LORD and against his Anointed One.
3"Let us break their chains," they say, "and throw off their fetters."

4The One enthroned in heaven laughs; the Lord scoffs at them.
5Then he rebukes them in his anger and terrifies them in his wrath, saying,
6"I have installed my King on Zion, my holy hill."

7I will proclaim the decree of the LORD:
He said to me, "You are my Son; today I have become your Father.
8Ask of me, and I will make the nations your inheritance, the ends of the earth your possession.
9You will rule them with an iron sceptre; you will dash them to pieces like pottery."

10Therefore, you kings, be wise; be warned, you rulers of the earth.
11Serve the LORD with fear and rejoice with trembling.
12Kiss the Son, lest he be angry and you be destroyed in your way, for his wrath can flare up in a moment. Blessed are all who take refuge in him.

Words: Heaven; Proclaim; Refuge; Sceptre; Sinful; Sovereignty; Worship; Wrath

Maps and Place Names: Zion

Boot Camp 003/Getting started with you
Boot Camp 004/Getting started with God

THINK ABOUT IT DAY 14
WHO RULES YOUR LIFE?

Who rules your ambitions? Who rules your words and intentions? The people in this Psalm want to rule themselves. They want to gather together and break off the rule of God over their lives. Why?

Because they are proud? Yes. Because they are stubborn? Certainly. Because they are sinful? Absolutely. You see, they are sinful and stupid enough to think that they actually can rule their own lives better than God can. They assume that they will make a better job of life if they get rid of God and put themselves on the throne.

So they see God's rule as a burden. They call it a chain. They don't see that in fact God's rule over them is their best hope. God is not a prison; he's a refuge. He's not to be opposed but to be worshipped. He's not to be got rid of but to be loved.

And since we can't actually get rid of God and one day we'll have to meet the one on the throne, we'd better learn to love his sovereignty now. It is, after all, the sovereignty of love, if only our proud, stubborn and sinful hearts would see it.

READ THIS THEN PRAY: The LORD is good, a refuge in times of trouble. He cares for those who trust in him (Nahum 1: 7).

Prayer: Lord God, you rule everything and are in charge of all the world and the universe. May I see you for who you truly are - the Sovereign Lord and my true refuge. I am truly safe in you alone - safe for all eternity. May you touch my heart today so that I will love you in return. Amen.

45

SECTION 4: TO WHOM WILL YOU LISTEN?

BIBLE READING
1 SAMUEL 25: 2-13

[2]A certain man in Maon, who had property there at Carmel, was very wealthy. He had a thousand goats and three thousand sheep, which he was shearing in Carmel. [3]His name was Nabal and his wife's name was Abigail. She was an intelligent and beautiful woman, but her husband, a Calebite, was surly and mean in his dealings.

[4]While David was in the desert, he heard that Nabal was shearing sheep. [5]So he sent ten young men and said to them, "Go up to Nabal at Carmel and greet him in my name. [6]Say to him: 'Long life to you! Good health to you and your household! And good health to all that is yours!

[7]Now I hear that it is sheep-shearing time. When your shepherds were with us, we did not ill-treat them, and the whole time they were at Carmel nothing of theirs was missing. [8]Ask your own servants and they will tell you. Therefore be favourable towards my young men, since we come at a festive time. Please give your servants and your son David whatever you can find for them.'"

[9]When David's men arrived, they gave Nabal this message in David's name. Then they waited.

[10]Nabal answered David's servants, "Who is this David? Who is this son of Jesse? Many servants are breaking away from their masters these days. [11]Why should I take my bread and water, and the meat I have slaughtered for my shearers, and give it to men coming from who knows where?"

[12]David's men turned round and went back. When they arrived, they reported every word. [13]David said to his men, "Put on your swords!" So they put on their swords, and David put on his. About four hundred men went up with David, while two hundred stayed with the supplies.

Who's Who: Abigail; Jesse; Nabal
Words: Grace

THINK ABOUT IT DAY 15
NABAL – THE FOOL

One of the most important skills of a leader is knowing who to listen to. That is, who to be shaped by, to take as a guiding voice. Over the next few days we'll look at some of the people that David listened to – or in Nabal's case, almost listened to.

Nabal's a horrid man: a mean and foolish bully who showed no grace at all and who was good at making enemies. So when David sends his very polite and reasonable request, Nabal's reply is typically rude. David's men report it word for word.

That's the crucial moment.

Will David be shaped by the rude fool? Will David silently, unconsciously allow Nabal to direct his attitudes and actions – deep down in his heart and mind? Will the fool turn David into a fool?

He almost does. Tomorrow we'll see that God rescues David from his own rash response, but were it not for that, David would have listened to the wrong man and ruined things for the future. "Put on your swords!" is the wrong thing to say.

Don't let fools wind you up. Don't let bad people turn you into the reflection of themselves. You're made in the image of God so listen to him.

Do not repay evil with evil or insult with insult, but with blessing, because to this you were called so that you may inherit a blessing (1 Peter 3: 9).

READ THIS THEN PRAY: Do not merely listen to the Word, and so deceive yourselves. Do what it says (James 1: 22).

Prayer: Father God, when people speak foolish things to me help me to be wise. Help me not to rush into actions rashly but instead listen to you and follow your advice. Amen.

49

BIBLE READING
1 SAMUEL 25: 14–35

[14]One of the servants told Nabal's wife, Abigail: "David sent messengers from the desert to give our master his greetings, but he hurled insults at them. [15]Yet these men were very good to us. They did not ill-treat us, and the whole time we were out in the fields near them nothing was missing. [16]Night and day they were a wall around us all the time we were herding our sheep near them. [17]Now think it over and see what you can do, because disaster is hanging over our master and his whole household. He is such a wicked man that no-one can talk to him."

[18]Abigail lost no time. She took two hundred loaves of bread, two skins of wine, five dressed sheep, five seahs of roasted grain, a hundred cakes of raisins and two hundred cakes of pressed figs, and loaded them on donkeys. [19]Then she told her servants, "Go on ahead; I'll follow you." But she did not tell her husband Nabal.

[20]As she came riding her donkey into a mountain ravine, there were David and his men descending towards her, and she met them. [21]David had just said, "It's been useless – all my watching over this fellow's property in the desert so that nothing of his was missing. He has paid me back evil for good. [22]May God deal with David, be it ever so severely, if by morning I leave alive one male of all who belong to him!"

[23]When Abigail saw David, she quickly got off her donkey and bowed down before David with her face to the ground. [24]She fell at his feet and said: "My lord, let the blame be on me alone. Please let your servant speak to you; hear what your servant has to say. [25]May my lord pay no attention to that wicked man Nabal. He is just like his name – his name is Fool, and folly goes with him. But as for me, your servant, I did not see the men my master sent.

[26]"Now since the LORD has kept you, my master, from bloodshed and from avenging yourself with your own hands, as surely as the LORD lives and as you live, may your enemies and all who intend to harm my master be like Nabal. [27]And let this gift, which your servant has brought to my master, be given to the men who follow you. [28]Please forgive your servant's offence, for the LORD will certainly make a lasting dynasty for my master, because he fights the LORD's battles. Let no wrongdoing be found in you as long as you live.

[29]Even though someone is pursuing you to take your life, the life of my master will be bound securely in the bundle of the living by the LORD your God. But the lives of your enemies he will hurl away as from the pocket of a sling. [30]When the LORD has done for my master every good thing he promised concerning him and has appointed him leader over Israel, [31]my master will not have on his conscience the staggering burden of needless bloodshed or of having avenged himself. And when the LORD has brought my master success, remember your servant."

[32]David said to Abigail, "Praise be to the LORD, the God of Israel, who has sent you today to meet me. [33]May you be blessed for your good judgment and for keeping me from bloodshed this day and from avenging myself with my own hands. [34]Otherwise, as surely as the LORD, the God of Israel, lives, who has kept me from harming you, if you had not come quickly to meet me, not one male belonging to Nabal would have been left alive by daybreak." [35]Then David accepted from her hand what she had brought to him and said, "Go home in peace. I have heard your words and granted your request."

WISDOM: Abigail was wise. She knew exactly what to do and did it. What does the Bible say about wisdom? It says that it is God who teaches us wisdom (Psalm 51: 6); respecting God is the beginning of wisdom (Psalm 111: 10); and if you want it, all you have to do is ask for it (James 1: 5). God's Word also teaches us that there is a difference between worldly wisdom and heavenly wisdom. Read James 3: 15–17.

Who's Who: Abigail; Nabal
Words: Praise; Seah; Skins

Boot Camp 004/Getting started with God

51

THINK ABOUT IT DAY 16
ABIGAIL – A GOOD WOMAN

Three points: Abigail spoke wisely and wasted no time. Intending to do good is no use at all if you don't act promptly. So if you see a helpful thing to do for someone, get on with it now! It might soon be too late.

David not only saw the error of his own ways and listened to the right person; he acknowledged that this good woman was sent by God. He heard the wisdom of God in her voice. Granted, she was beautiful and clever, but David saw the Lord in her.

There's a common understanding between David and Abigail: the Lord's character is their standard, the Lord's will is their hope and the Lord who hears is the one to whom they are accountable. No wonder they hit it off and end up married!

Don't fall in love with someone who doesn't have that common understanding with you.

READ THIS THEN PRAY: For the foolishness of God is wiser than man's wisdom and the weakness of God is stronger than man's strength (1 Corinthians 1: 25).

Prayer: Lord God, you now what is best for my life. May my life honour you and may those in my family also be people who love and trust in you. May you give me wisdom in choosing a wife or husband. May I only choose someone who believes in you and obeys you. Even if I never marry, Lord, I know that when my life belongs to you I will never be alone. Give me a love for your Word and a deep love for your person. In your name. Amen.

Zone in on Map

See full map of Israel on page 127 and
Place name index on pages 128–130
to find out more information on the following places:

Bethlehem
Judah
Jerusalem

To find out more about these places look up the following
scripture verses:

Bethlehem – Genesis 35:19; Ruth 1:1–2; Ruth 1:19–22; Micah
5:2; Matthew 2:1

Judah: Joshua 11:21; Joshua 15:1; Ruth 1:7; 1 Kings 12:20–21;
Lamentations 1:3; Daniel 1: 1–6; Matthew 2:6

Jerusalem: Joshua 10:1–5; 1 Kings 1:42; 2 Kings 25:8–12; Ezra
1:5; Nehemiah 2:17; Matthew 16:21; Acts 6:7

BIBLE READING
2 SAMUEL 3: 17–31

[17]Abner conferred with the elders of Israel and said, "For some time you have wanted to make David your king. [18]Now do it! For the LORD promised David, `By my servant David I will rescue my people Israel from the hand of the Philistines and from the hand of all their enemies.'" [19]Abner also spoke to the Benjamites in person. Then he went to Hebron to tell David everything that Israel and the whole house of Benjamin wanted to do. [20]When Abner, who had twenty men with him, came to David at Hebron, David prepared a feast for him and his men. [21]Then Abner said to David, "Let me go at once and assemble all Israel for my lord the king, so that they may make a compact with you, and that you may rule over all that your heart desires." So David sent Abner away, and he went in peace.

[22]Just then David's men and Joab returned from a raid and brought with them a great deal of plunder. But Abner was no longer with David in Hebron, because David had sent him away, and he had gone in peace. [23]When Joab and all the soldiers with him arrived, he was told that, Abner, son of Ner, had come to the king and that the king had sent him away and that he had gone in peace.

[24]So Joab went to the king and said, "What have you done? Look, Abner came to you. Why did you let him go? Now he is gone! [25]You know Abner son of Ner; he came to deceive you and observe your movements and find out everything you are doing." [26]Joab then left David and sent messengers after Abner, and they brought him back from the well of Sirah. But David did not know it. [27]Now when Abner returned to Hebron, Joab took him aside...as though to speak with him privately. And there, to avenge the blood of his brother, Asahel, Joab stabbed him in the stomach, and he died.

[28]Later, when David heard about this, he said, "I and my kingdom are for ever innocent before the LORD concerning the blood of Abner son of Ner. [29]May his blood fall upon the head of Joab and upon all his father's house! May Joab's house never be without someone who has a running sore or leprosy or who leans on a crutch or who falls by the sword or who lacks food."

[30](Joab and his brother, Abishai, murdered Abner because he had killed their brother, Asahel, in the battle of Gibeon.)

[31]Then David said to Joab and all the people with him, "Tear your clothes and put on sackcloth and walk in mourning in front of Abner." King David himself walked behind the bier.

THINK ABOUT IT DAY 17
JOAB – THE HATER

Joab was David's general and Abner had been Saul's general. After Saul's death, civil war broke out between the house of Saul and the house of David. In the war Abner had been pursued by Joab's brother, Asahel. Abner pleaded with the younger and less experienced Asahel not to chase him but Asahel wouldn't listen; in the ensuing fight, Abner killed Asahel. Abner deeply wanted peace; he was happy for David to be king over a united Israel; so he bravely joined David's men. David had welcomed him in the Lord's name.

David wanted the peace of the Lord to be enjoyed in the kingdom. Abner sought peace. But Joab wanted revenge. Joab wanted a blood-feud. His heart was full of hatred so he wanted 'honour killings'. He wasn't interested in mercy; he couldn't care less about what the God of peace wanted. He despised God's law and became a murderer.

Sadly, you'll find people like Joab wherever you go: haters whose hearts care nothing for God's ways of mercy and peace. They always cause arguments and trouble. Stay away from them if you can. If you can't, don't listen to them. Either way, never let your heart fill up with anger or revenge. Leave grudges behind; pursue God's peace.

READ THIS THEN PRAY: Blessed is the man who always fears the LORD, but he who hardens his heart falls into trouble (Proverbs 28: 14).

Prayer: Lord God, give me open ears to listen to your Word. May I pay more attention to you than to people who do not care for your ways. Help me to follow your example of forgiveness instead of holding grudges. Thank you that you have not treated me in the way that I deserve - your mercy is amazing. I am thankful that you are such a gracious God. Amen.

Who's Who: Abishai; Abner; Asahel; Benjamites; Joab; Ner; Philistines
Words: Bier; Sackcloth
Maps and Place Names: Hebron; Well of Sirah

BIBLE READING
2 SAMUEL 5: 1-5

All the tribes of Israel came to David at Hebron and said, "We are your own flesh and blood. [2]In the past, while Saul was king over us, you were the one who led Israel on their military campaigns. And the LORD said to you, 'You shall shepherd my people Israel, and you shall become their ruler.'" [3]When all the elders of Israel had come to King David at Hebron, the king made a compact with them at Hebron before the LORD, and they anointed David king over Israel. [4]David was thirty years old when he became king, and he reigned for forty years. [5]In Hebron he reigned over Judah for seven years and six months, and in Jerusalem he reigned over all Israel and Judah for thirty-three years.

SERVE GOD: As Christians when we serve others we serve God. When we put others first before ourselves we are doing what God desires us to do. In 1 Peter 4: 9-11 it says, 'Offer hospitality to one another without grumbling. Each one should use whatever gift he has received to serve others, faithfully administering God's grace in its various forms.' In Ephesians 6: 7 we are told that we are to 'serve wholeheartedly, as if you were serving the Lord, not men.' So do whatever you can for others and do it without complaint. Be enthusiastic about helping and giving to others – and when you serve and work for others just think about this – it's actually Jesus you are doing it for!

THINK ABOUT IT DAY 18
GOOD MEN – GOD'S PROMISE

What keeps you going in God's ways even when it's difficult?

Well, Christians down the years have found that God's promises are to be trusted. God doesn't always deliver on his promises straightaway: sometimes we have to be patient and wait until the right time. But he always keeps his promises.

After seven years and six months of civil war, and all the time before that when Saul was chasing David for his life, David was finally crowned king.

He listened to the good men who came to him. They recognized the right time. They approached David. David didn't seize the crown for himself. They reminded him of God's promises to him and of God's work for him: "And the Lord said to you ..."

We need to listen to good people who encourage us to serve God in some new way when they remind us of God's promises. They didn't say, "You can do it, you're brilliant!" They pointed David to God and reminded him to trust his promises. Such people should be the ones to shape our lives. And we should be that kind of person to others.

READ THIS THEN PRAY: You know with all your heart and soul that not one of all the good promises the LORD your God gave you has failed (Joshua 21: 45).

Prayer: Lord God, I ask you to send me godly people to teach me how to live and honour you. May these people shape my life in a way that pleases you. Make me willing to learn so that I may teach others about you too. In your name. Amen.

Words: Grace
Maps and Place Names: Hebron; Jerusalem; Judah

BIBLE READING
2 SAMUEL 5: 6-12

[6]The king and his men marched to Jerusalem to attack the Jebusites, who lived there. The Jebusites said to David, "You will not get in here; even the blind and the lame can ward you off." They thought, "David cannot get in here." [7]Nevertheless, David captured the fortress of Zion, the City of David.

[8]On that day, David said, "Anyone who conquers the Jebusites will have to use the water shaft to reach those 'lame and blind' who are David's enemies." That is why they say, "The 'blind and lame' will not enter the palace."

[9]David then took up residence in the fortress and called it the City of David. He built up the area around it, from the supporting terraces inward. [10]And he became more and more powerful, because the LORD God Almighty was with him.

[11]Now Hiram king of Tyre sent messengers to David, along with cedar logs and carpenters and stonemasons, and they built a palace for David. [12]And David knew that the LORD had established him as king over Israel and had exalted his kingdom for the sake of his people Israel.

JERUSALEM: This was also called the City of David once David had made it the capital city of his kingdom. But the City of Jerusalem and the area around it has a bit of history before David and a future after him. The history is that Abraham was sent by God to Mount Moriah to offer up his son, Isaac, as a sacrifice – but in the end God provided another sacrifice instead and Isaac was saved. It is interesting to note that Mount Moriah is in the same area as Jerusalem. Many years later God would offer up his own Son, the Lord Jesus, as a sacrifice for the sin of his people. That would be outside the city walls of Jersualem on a hill called Calvary.

Who's Who: Hiram: King of Tyre; Jebusites; Moses
Words: Ark of the Covenant; Established; Exalted; Praise
Maps and Place Names: Bethlehem; Jerusalem; Tyre

Think About It Day 19
Jerusalem at Last!

At long last!

After the dangers, the battles, the waiting, David takes Jerusalem and makes it the capital of Israel. At last he can establish a centre for a kingdom that will spread the wisdom and truth of God over the surrounding nations. At last he has a place to call home – something he hasn't had since he left his father's farm in Bethlehem all those years ago. His time in 'God's Difficult School' draws to an end; the preparation is over.

But Jerusalem wasn't just David's city. Centuries earlier God had kept saying to his people through Moses that he would have a place where "he would make his name to dwell". It would be the place where all Israel should gather to worship him: the focal point of the life of God's people. So it's also God's city, God's homecoming, which is why David has the ark of the covenant brought to Jerusalem in the next chapter.

When God blesses your life, it's for your enjoyment and for the glory of his name. The good things that he gives you are for the praise of the one who dwells in your life as he dwelt in Jerusalem and who wants your life to be a centre for worship. Make your life his home.

READ THIS THEN PRAY: I eagerly expect and hope that I will in no way be ashamed, but will have sufficient courage so that now as always Christ will be exalted in my body, whether by life or by death (Philippians 1: 20).

Prayer: Lord God, thank you for the times you have blessed me with good things. Please help me to allow you to be the centre of my life and worship. In your name. Amen.

BIBLE READINGS
LUKE2: 39–40 & 52
MATTHEW 13: 52–56
ISAIAH 50: 4–5

LUKE 2: 39–40

39When Joseph and Mary had done everything required by the Law of the Lord, they returned to Galilee to their own town of Nazareth. 40And the child grew and became strong; he was filled with wisdom, and the grace of God was upon him.

LUKE 2: 52

And Jesus grew in wisdom and stature, and in favour with God and men.

MATTHEW 13: 52–56

52He said to them, "Therefore every teacher of the law who has been instructed about the kingdom of heaven is like the owner of a house who brings out of his storeroom new treasures as well as old." 53When Jesus had finished these parables, he moved on from there. 54Coming to his home town, he began teaching the people in their synagogue, and they were amazed. "Where did this man get this wisdom and these miraculous powers?" they asked. 55"Isn't this the carpenter's son? Isn't his mother's name Mary, and aren't his brothers James, Joseph, Simon and Judas? 56Aren't all his sisters with us? Where then did this man get all these things?"

ISAIAH 50: 4–5

4The Sovereign LORD has given me an instructed tongue, to know the Word that sustains the weary. He wakens me morning by morning, wakens my ear to listen like one being taught. 5The Sovereign LORD has opened my ears, and I have not been rebellious; I have not drawn back.

Think About It Day 20
Jesus is Wise

Jesus knew who to listen to. He knew that among all the voices that surrounded him, telling to be this or do that there was one true voice: the voice of his Father in heaven. He could have let his life be shaped by those who shouted the loudest, flattered him the most or threatened him the fiercest. He could have adopted the wisdom of the day. But he listened to his Father's will. Isaiah prophesied that God's true and great servant would listen like one being taught, and listening he would obey even if it meant pain and loss.

We have the same Father who speaks to us by the Spirit through his Word, the Bible. There are many people who would like to direct and control your life; and the world still has its so-called 'wisdom'. But you can be truly wise by listening to God's Word and to those whose speech is guided by it. Let that be the teacher and guide throughout your life. Especially today.

READ THIS THEN PRAY: You guide me with your counsel, and afterward you will take me into glory (Psalm 73: 24).

Prayer: Lord God, I thank you for your Word, the Bible and for the fact that your spirit speaks to me through it. Please control my life today and always and make me willing to follow your direction. In your name. Amen.

Words: Prophesy; Sovereignty; Stature; Sustain; Synagogue

Boot Camp 004/Getting started with God
Boot Camp 005/Getting started with Jesus Christ

61

BIBLE READING
PSALM 24

Of David. A psalm.
The earth is the LORD's, and everything in it,
the world, and all who live in it;
[2]for he founded it upon the seas and established it upon the waters.

[3]Who may ascend the hill of the LORD?
Who may stand in his holy place?
[4]He who has clean hands and a pure heart,
who does not lift up his soul to an idol or swear by what is false.
[5]He will receive blessing from the LORD
and vindication from God his Saviour.
[6]Such is the generation of those who seek him,
who seek your face, O God of Jacob. Selah

[7]Lift up your heads, O you gates;
be lifted up, you ancient doors,
that the King of glory may come in.
[8]Who is this King of glory?
The LORD strong and mighty,
the LORD mighty in battle.
[9]Lift up your heads, O you gates;
lift them up, you ancient doors,
that the King of glory may come in.
[10]Who is he, this King of glory?
The LORD Almighty –
he is the King of glory. Selah

Words: House of God; Saviour; Selah; Vindication

Boot Camp 001/Getting started with the Old Testament
Boot Camp 004/Getting started with God

THINK ABOUT IT DAY 21
HOW WILL YOU DRAW
NEAR TO GOD?

David knew that God is holy, so he asks the question "How can we draw near to him and live with him?" How can we "ascend the hill of the Lord"? Our hands (the things we do) are not totally clean; our hearts (the things that we want) are not all pure; and what we say is not always right.

However, the Lord himself has done battle for us. Jesus has fought against sin, sinfulness and Satan for us. Like the great returning warrior that he is, Jesus has gone up to the presence of God and the gates of God's city have been flung wide for him. David the king speaks in a way that points us to the greatest king, the King of Glory. Because he is clean, pure and right towards God, and because he is our leader, we can draw near to God with him. Because he goes into God's presence, so can we. Your fellowship with the Holy One all rests on Jesus. He's your new and living way to the Father. You have access to the Father, so make the approach.

Therefore, brothers, since we have confidence to enter the Most Holy Place by the blood of Jesus, [20]by a new and living way opened for us through the curtain, that is, his body, [21]and since we have a great priest over the house of God, [22]let us draw near to God with a sincere heart in full assurance of faith, having our hearts sprinkled to cleanse us from a guilty conscience and having our bodies washed with pure water (Hebrews 10: 19–22).

READ THIS THEN PRAY: I cry out in distress and he hears my voice. He ransoms me unharmed from the battle waged against me, even though many oppose me. God, who is enthroned forever, will hear them and afflict them - men who never change their ways and have no fear of God (Psalm 55: 17–19).

Prayer: Lord God, give me a longing today to be with you, close to you, as I come to you in prayer. Thank you for the gift of your Son, the Lord Jesus. Your Word tells me that he is the only way to you and to eternal life. I thank you that your love has made it possible for me to be with you. Amen.

SECTION 5: GOLDEN DAYS OF GRACE

DAY 22: 2 SAMUEL 5: 17–25

TRUST GOD WHEN YOU CAN DO IT YOURSELF

DAY 23: 2 SAMUEL 6: 17–19

WHEN GOD CAME HOME

DAY 24: 2 SAMUEL 7: 8–16

GOD'S AMAZING PROMISE

DAY 25: 2 SAMUEL 9: 1–11

REFLECTING GOD

DAY 26: 2 SAMUEL 8: 1–15

VICTORY AFTER VICTORY

DAY 27: REVELATION 19: 11–16

JESUS IS THE GREATEST KING

DAY 28: PSALM 103

PRAISE THE LORD!

BIBLE READING
2 SAMUEL 5: 17-25

[17]When the Philistines heard that David had been anointed king over Israel, they went up in full force to search for him, but David heard about it and went down to the stronghold. [18]Now the Philistines had come and spread out in the Valley of Rephaim; [19]so David enquired of the LORD, "Shall I go and attack the Philistines? Will you hand them over to me?"
The LORD answered him, "Go, for I will surely hand the Philistines over to you."
[20]So David went to Baal Perazim, and there he defeated them. He said, "As waters break out, the LORD has broken out against my enemies before me." So that place was called Baal Perazim. [21]The Philistines abandoned their idols there, and David and his men carried them off.
[22]Once more the Philistines came up and spread out in the Valley of Rephaim; [23]so David enquired of the LORD, and he answered, "Do not go straight up, but circle round behind them and attack them in front of the balsam trees. [24]As soon as you hear the sound of marching in the tops of the balsam trees, move quickly, because that will mean the LORD has gone out in front of you to strike the Philistine army." [25]So David did as the LORD commanded him, and he struck down the Philistines all the way from Gibeon to Gezer.

Who's Who: Philistines
Words: Idols; Balsam
Maps and Place Names: Baal Perazim; Gezer; Gibeon; Valley of Rephaim

THINK ABOUT IT DAY 22
TRUST GOD WHEN YOU
CAN DO IT YOURSELF

One small point first. Notice the teamwork. God 'broke out' against the Philistines, but 'David...defeated them'. God's is the great power, but he calls us to work with him and one another as he builds his kingdom. It's teamwork.

Now the main point.

Twice, Israel's worst enemy at the time attacked David's new kingdom and throne. Twice David checked with God, asking "What am I supposed to do Lord?" Twice God said that he would defeat the Philistines and twice he did it.

David was naturally good at battles and he specialized in beating Philistines. He'd been beating them since the fight with Goliath. But he doesn't trust himself. He's confident, but not self-confident. He takes the time to turn to God for guidance.

We are at our most vulnerable when we are doing well. That's the time when we forget to involve God in our decisions and fail to trust him for a good outcome. But when David was doing well in these golden days, he trusted God for victory. And so did Jesus. He only ever did what his Father wanted him to do. He could easily have done anything he wanted, but always preferred to do His Father's will.

Believe in yourself? Better to believe in God.

READ THIS THEN PRAY: But the Lord is faithful, and he will strengthen and protect you from the evil one (2 Thessalonians 3: 3).

Prayer: Lord God, I need help and protection from those who wish to harm me. But I also need protection when things are going well. I need you to deliver me from temptation. Help me not to give in when I find that my heart wants to take my body into sin. May I never forget to bring my plans and ambitions to you - to seek your will and your advice. In your name. Amen.

BIBLE READING
2 SAMUEL 6: 17-19

[17]They brought the ark of the LORD and set it in its place inside the tent that David had pitched for it, and David sacrificed burnt offerings and fellowship offerings before the LORD. [18]After he had finished sacrificing the burnt offerings and fellowship offerings, he blessed the people in the name of the LORD Almighty. [19]Then he gave a loaf of bread, a cake of dates and a cake of raisins to each person in the whole crowd of Israelites, both men and women. And all the people went to their homes.

THE EXODUS: Exodus means 'a going out' and is the name of the second book of the Old Testament. This book describes the time when the Hebrew people left Egypt and slavery to journey to the land that God had promised their forefathers Abraham, Isaac and Jacob. The Israelites arrived at the Promised Land, under the leadership of Moses. Joshua and Caleb were sent to spy out the land with some other men. They gave a good account of the land but the other spies didn't. The people chose to believe the negative report even though God had told them to take the Promised Land. They failed to trust that he was stronger than the awesome looking people that they saw. The Israelites were therefore banished to the desert for another forty years. When the forty years had passed and it was time to enter into the Promised Land, Joshua and Caleb were the only ones who were left alive from the original number. Even Moses was dead.

THINK ABOUT IT DAY 23
WHEN GOD CAME HOME

The ark was the visible sign from the days of the Exodus that God was among his people. God wasn't in the wooden, gold-covered box, but it was the way that everyone could see that the loving, holy God was among his people. It had to be in Jerusalem, the place that God would make his name to dwell. It was right that David should have brought it up to the city.

Its progress was marred by the death of Uzzah, who reached out to touch it even though God told everyone not to. God is Holy: don't mess with him!

There was also great joy, with music and singing and dancing! And here we read that there was a lot of generosity.

God's presence among us should make us think of his holiness so that we respect him (fear his holy name) and think of him with awe. It should also mean joyful worship. But it should also make us generous with what God has given us. We are blessed so that others might be blessed through us. If the Holy One is with you and you truly rejoice in it, it will show by the way that you generously bless the people around you.

READ THIS THEN PRAY: Who among the gods is like you, O LORD? Who is like you–majestic in holiness, awesome in glory, working wonders (Exodus 15: 10–12)?

Prayer: Lord God, you are holy - without sin, yet you have shown your love to sinners by sending your son Jesus Christ to die for them. Help me to understand that I am a sinner and in need of your mercy. Your Word tells me to be generous with what I have. Help me to be willing to share and may I always thank you for what you have given me. Every good and perfect gift comes from you. I pray this in your name. Amen.

Who's Who: Uzzah
Words: Ark of the LORD; Bless; Burnt offerings; Fellowship offerings; Holy

BIBLE READING
2 SAMUEL 7: 8-16

[8]"Now then, tell my servant David, 'This is what the LORD Almighty says: I took you from the pasture and from following the flock to be ruler over my people Israel. [9]I have been with you wherever you have gone, and I have cut off all your enemies from before you. Now I will make your name great, like the names of the greatest men of the earth. [10]And I will provide a place for my people Israel and will plant them so that they can have a home of their own and no longer be disturbed. Wicked people shall not oppress them any more, as they did at the beginning [11]and have done ever since the time I appointed leaders over my people Israel. I will also give you rest from all your enemies.

The LORD declares to you that the LORD himself will establish a house for you: [12]When your days are over and you rest with your fathers, I will raise up your offspring to succeed you, who will come from your own body, and I will establish his kingdom. [13]He is the one who will build a house for my Name, and I will establish the throne of his kingdom for ever. [14]I will be his father, and he shall be my son. When he does wrong, I will punish him with the rod of men, with floggings inflicted by men. [15]But my love will never be taken away from him, as I took it away from Saul, whom I removed from before you. [16]Your house and your kingdom shall endure for ever before me; your throne shall be established for ever.'"

THE PROMISED SAVIOUR: In the very first chapters of the Bible we read about the first sin and the first promise of a Saviour. Read Genesis 3:14-15. Here God is telling the devil that the future holds a sure and certain defeat for him. A human being will defeat him. Jesus Christ who is both God and man is the fulfilment of this promise.

Who's Who: Isaiah; Jesus; Saul; Solomon
Words: Cut off; Offspring
Maps and Place Names: Judah

THINK ABOUT IT DAY 24 GOD'S AMAZING PROMISE

Wow! What a promise!

The eternal king, who will cause God's Kingdom to grow and last forever, will come from David's line of descendents. David wanted to build a house for God, but God was going to build a house for David!

The promises are sort-of fulfilled in the life of Solomon, but even Solomon, despite all his greatness, died. And the kingdoms of Israel and then later of Judah passed away. (Who's the King of Judah now? There's no throne in the physical city of Jerusalem.) God is saying that out of David's line the eternal king of a heavenly kingdom will come. And God will do the whole thing; David couldn't make it happen.

We like to think that we can do great things for God, which is good. But we need to remember that God has promised to do even greater things for us and for his own name.

God kept his promise to David: Jesus, 'Son of David', is the eternal king. God will keep his promises to you too.

 READ THIS THEN PRAY: All of us have become like one who is unclean, and all our righteous acts are like filthy rags; we all shrivel up like a leaf, and like the wind our sins sweep us away (Isaiah 64: 6).

Prayer: Lord God, I know that even the good things I do aren't good enough to save me from sin. It is only Christ's death that has the power to save. Show me how inadequate I am. Without you sin will sweep me away. Make my heart turn to you for forgiveness so that you can shape my life into one that honours you. Amen.

71

BIBLE READING
2 SAMUEL 9: 1–11

David asked, "Is there anyone still left of the house of Saul to whom I can show kindness for Jonathan's sake?" [2]Now there was a servant of Saul's household named Ziba. They called him to appear before David, and the king said to him, "Are you Ziba?" "Your servant," he replied. [3]The king asked, "Is there no one still left of the house of Saul to whom I can show God's kindness?" Ziba answered the king, "There is still a son of Jonathan; he is crippled in both feet." [4]"Where is he?" the king asked. Ziba answered, "He is at the house of Makir, son of Ammiel in Lo Debar." [5]So King David had him brought from Lo Debar, from the house of Makir son of Ammiel. [6]When Mephibosheth, son of Jonathan, the son of Saul, came to David, he bowed down to pay him honour. David said, "Mephibosheth!" "Your servant," he replied. [7]"Don't be afraid," David said to him, "for I will surely show you kindness for the sake of your father Jonathan. I will restore to you all the land that belonged to your grandfather Saul, and you will always eat at my table." [8]Mephibosheth bowed down and said, "What is your servant, that you should notice a dead dog like me?" [9]Then the king summoned Ziba, Saul's servant, and said to him, "I have given your master's grandson everything that belonged to Saul and his family. [10]You and your sons and your servants are to farm the land for him and bring in the crops, so that your master's grandson may be provided for. And Mephibosheth, grandson of your master, will always eat at my table." (Now Ziba had fifteen sons and twenty servants.) [11]Then Ziba said to the king, "Your servant will do whatever my lord the king commands his servant to do." So Mephibosheth ate at David's table like one of the king's sons.

Who's Who: Ammiel; Jonathan; Makir; Mephibosheth; Saul; Ziba

Maps and Place Names: Lo Debar

THINK ABOUT IT DAY 25
REFLECTING GOD

David owed Mephibosheth nothing. Mephibosheth had done nothing for David and could offer him nothing. But David had made a promise to Mephibosheth's father, Jonathan. And for Jonathan's sake he blessed his crippled son.

No one knew about that promise, by the way. Except God. When David had promised to remember Jonathan's 'house' he and Jonathan were in the presence of God who hears everything. David's heart was full of kindness, loyalty, love and the proper fear of God. He knew that God had heard the promise and he knew that he was answerable to God.

David, who had received such a wonderful promise from God, becomes a promise-keeper himself. He could trust God's Word, so his own word becomes trustworthy.

Do you see what's happening? He's beginning to rule his Kingdom in a way that reflects God's character. He's beginning to be God's King, governing in God's way, who shows God's people what God is like so that they might truly live as God's people should.

That's the kind of thing that Jesus wants to do in your life – make you a reflection of him, so that people can look at you and see what he is like.

READ THIS THEN PRAY: As water reflects a face, so a man's heart reflects the man (Proverbs 27: 19). And we, who with unveiled faces all reflect the Lord's glory, are being transformed into his likeness with ever-increasing glory, which comes from the Lord (2 Corinthians 3: 18).

Prayer: Lord God, my life of sin does not reflect you as you are holy and sinless. Turn me away from sin towards you. May your righteousness be seen in my life. Make me your child so that I will reflect back to others a family resemblance. May those who don't know you see your beauty when they see my life. Amen.

BIBLE READING
2 SAMUEL 8: 1–15

In the course of time, David defeated the Philistines and subdued them, and he took Metheg Ammah from the control of the Philistines. [2]David also defeated the Moabites. He made them lie down on the ground and measured them off with a length of cord. Every two lengths of them were put to death, and the third length was allowed to live. So the Moabites became subject to David and brought tribute. [3]Moreover, David fought Hadadezer son of Rehob, king of Zobah, when he went to restore his control along the Euphrates River. [4]David captured a thousand of his chariots, seven thousand charioteers and twenty thousand foot soldiers. He hamstrung all but a hundred of the chariot horses. [5]When the Arameans of Damascus came to help Hadadezer, king of Zobah, David struck down twenty-two thousand of them. [6]He put garrisons in the Aramean kingdom of Damascus, and the Arameans became subject to him and brought tribute. The LORD gave David victory wherever he went. [7]David took the gold shields that belonged to the officers of Hadadezer and brought them to Jerusalem. [8]From Tebah and Berothai, towns that belonged to Hadadezer, King David took a great quantity of bronze. [9]When Tou, king of Hamath, heard that David had defeated the entire army of Hadadezer, [10]he sent his son, Joram, to King David to greet him and congratulate him on his victory in battle over Hadadezer, who had been at war with Tou. Joram brought with him articles of silver and gold and bronze. [11]King David dedicated these articles to the LORD, as he had done with the silver and gold from all the nations he had subdued: [12]Edom and Moab, the Ammonites and the Philistines, and Amalek. He also dedicated the plunder taken from Hadadezer, son of Rehob, king of Zobah. [13]And David became famous after he returned from striking down eighteen thousand Edomites in the Valley of Salt. [14]He put garrisons throughout Edom, and all the Edomites became subject to David. The LORD gave David victory wherever he went. [15]David reigned over all Israel, doing what was just and right for all his people.

THINK ABOUT IT DAY 26
VICTORY AFTER VICTORY

As David reigns in a godly way his kingdom increases. In fact, it's really God's reign that's extending over the surrounding nations.

People who have been hostile to Israel and to the Lord are now under the leadership of God's anointed king. God's law goes out from Jerusalem to govern the lives of more and more people – people whose lives were once lived in rebellion against God. God's truth is now taught over a far wider area. God is known and worshipped by those who only ever heard about false gods. Kindness and grace flow from the throne in Jerusalem to more countries. God's true and righteous judgements fall on a wider area. The boundaries of God's rule are spreading.

David is not indulging in a bit of proud empire-building for himself. He's extending God's influence with victory after victory.

You and I are involved in the same thing – not by fighting people but by fighting sin; not with swords but with the gospel. David deeply wanted God's kingdom to grow and he was full of zeal for it. Same with Jesus. What about you?

READ THIS THEN PRAY: If you do what is right, will you not be accepted? But if you do not do what is right, sin is crouching at your door; it desires to have you, but you must master it (Genesis 4: 7).

Prayer: Lord God, you are a merciful and forgiving God. As a sinner I need your forgiveness. Change my heart from one that fights against your will to one that fights against sin. Only you can change me in this way. May my sin not be in charge of the direction that my life takes. You are my master. Everything belongs to you. I pray that you will open my eyes so that I will realise what this means for my life now and in eternity. Amen.

Who's Who: Moabites; Philistines
Words: Eternity; Garrison; Godly; Gospel; Grace; Hamstrung; Subject; Tribute; Zeal
Maps and Place Names: Metheg Ammah

75

BIBLE READING
REVELATION 19: 11-16

[11]I saw heaven standing open and there before me was a white horse, whose rider is called Faithful and True. With justice he judges and makes war. [12]His eyes are like blazing fire, and on his head are many crowns. He has a name written on him that no one knows but he himself. [13]He is dressed in a robe dipped in blood, and his name is the Word of God. [14]The armies of heaven were following him, riding on white horses and dressed in fine linen, white and clean. [15]Out of his mouth comes a sharp sword with which to strike down the nations. "He will rule them with an iron sceptre." He treads the winepress of the fury of the wrath of God Almighty. [16]On his robe and on his thigh he has this name written: KING OF KINGS AND LORD OF LORDS.

TREADING THE WINEPRESS: People in Bible times were familiar with farming and rural life. They lived in a warm climate and as a result had the perfect conditions to grow vineyards. Therefore, words that may not be that familiar to you today were actually very familiar to Bible listeners and readers back then. The words treading the winepress, for them would conjur up a picture of a man in a large vat stamping on the grapes that had just been harvested in order to squeeze out the juice. It was hard back-breaking work. Here the words treading the winepress are used to describe Christ's work. He is the only one who has fully taken on the wrath of God on the cross at Calvary. We will never understand how hard this work was for him. However, he will not always be Saviour. To those who reject him, one day he will be Judge and God's wrath will be administered to God's enemies by the King of kings and Lord of lords.

THINK ABOUT IT DAY 27
JESUS THE GREATEST KING

What a striking picture of Jesus! He is riding a white horse, like a victorious Roman general returning from battle to crowds of cheering citizens. He wages war on the nations that are opposed to him. He commands a vast army wearing clean white linen to show that they are pure and righteous. His own robe is dipped in blood for his battles have been fierce. His name is the Word of God, showing that all God's will is done through him. He wears many crowns for he rules over many nations and multiplied power rests on his head. Everything that he says is faithful and true – no lies, no 'spin', no half-truths with this king. He has another name, another 'handle': King of kings and Lord of lords.

Who is this? It's Jesus, the greatest king. Are you one of the cheering citizens of heaven who are glad to see his rule extend? Are you delighted that he reigns, having conquered sin for you? Or does something in you secretly wish that even at the end of time there will still be some opposition to him? Do you really want him to win? He has won.

READ THIS THEN PRAY: How awesome is the LORD Most High, the great King over all the earth (Pslam 47: 2)!

Prayer: Lord Jesus, you are the greatest king. Even those who do not worship you will one day bow the knee before you. Draw my heart towards you and make me one of those who loves you and cheers for your victory. Amen.

Words: Faithful; Justice; Heaven; Wrath
God's Names: Faithful and True; King of kings and Lord of lords

77

BIBLE READING
PSALM 103

Of David.
Praise the LORD, O my soul; all my inmost being, praise his holy name. [2]Praise the LORD, O my soul, and forget not all his benefits – [3]who forgives all your sins and heals all your diseases, [4]who redeems your life from the pit and crowns you with love and compassion, [5]who satisfies your desires with good things so that your youth is renewed like the eagle's. [6]The LORD works righteousness and justice for all the oppressed. [7]He made known his ways to Moses, his deeds to the people of Israel: [8]The LORD is compassionate and gracious, slow to anger, abounding in love. [9]He will not always accuse, nor will he harbour his anger for ever; [10]he does not treat us as our sins deserve or repay us according to our iniquities. [11]For as high as the heavens are above the earth, so great is his love for those who fear him; [12]as far as the east is from the west, so far has he removed our transgressions from us. [13]As a father has compassion on his children, so the LORD has compassion on those who fear him; [14]for he knows how we are formed, he remembers that we are dust. [15]As for man, his days are like grass, he flourishes like a flower of the field; [16]the wind blows over it and it is gone, and its place remembers it no more. [17]But from everlasting to everlasting the LORD's love is with those who fear him, and his righteousness with their children's children- [18]with those who keep his covenant and remember to obey his precepts. [19]The LORD has established his throne in heaven, and his kingdom rules over all. [20]Praise the LORD, you his angels, you mighty ones who do his bidding, who obey his Word. [21]Praise the LORD, all his heavenly hosts, you his servants who do his will. [22]Praise the LORD, all his works everywhere in his dominion. Praise the LORD, O my soul.

AS FAR AS EAST IS DISTANT FROM THE WEST: This distance is immeasurable – check it out for yourself on a globe. No matter how far west you go – you can always go further west. So how far has God removed our sins from those who trust in him? If you get out your ruler or tape measure you will never ever be able to measure that distance! It's impossible!

THINK ABOUT IT DAY 28
PRAISE THE LORD!

See how David praises God for being such a wonderful, almighty king for his people. How great is our God – let David's praise lift your heart today.

Look at the things that God does: he forgives all your sins (I love that word 'all'!). He heals our diseases; he pays the price for our release from the grip of death; he glorifies and honours us with his love; he satisfies our souls with good things, not rubbish.

Look at his heart: he's always thinking of you and he understands your weaknesses; he is full of compassion for you; he is faithful in love and faithful to his promises. This is how he will govern your life from his eternal throne. No one else will ever be this good to you – ever. If you're his, no one can ever separate you from this love – ever. So yes, we will praise him and we do think he's so wonderful that all creation, in heaven and on the earth, should be praising him. Praise the Lord!

READ THIS THEN PRAY: For we do not have a high priest who is unable to sympathize with our weaknesses, but we have one who has been tempted in every way, just as we are—yet was without sin (Hebrews 4: 15).

Prayer: Lord God, you have given me so much - my daily food, drink, clothes, my family... You give the gift of eternal life to those who trust in your Son. I need all these things - I am weak without food and drink, I am cold and needy without clothes and the love of others. I am lost without your salvation. Thank you for understanding me in my weaknesses and sympathising with me. Amen.

Words: Angels; Compassion; Faithful; Forgives; Glorifies; Gracious; Iniquities; Heavenly hosts; Praise

SECTION 6: DARK DAYS OF SIN

DAY 29: DEUTERONOMY 17: 14–17;
2 SAMUEL 11: 1–4

THE FATAL WEAKNESS

DAY 30: 2 SAMUEL 11: 1–5

HOW NOT TO HANDLE TEMPTATION:

GIVE IN

DAY 31: 2 SAMUEL 11: 6–17

HOW NOT TO HANDLE SIN:

COVER UP

DAY 32: 2 SAMUEL 11: 26–12: 7

HOW NOT TO HANDLE GUILT: DENY IT

DAY 33: 2 SAMUEL 12: 7–24

GOD WOUNDS AND HEALS

DAY 34: 2 CORINTHIANS 5: 21;
1 PETER 2: 21–25

JESUS IS PURE

DAY 35: PSALM 51

WHAT GOD DESIRES FROM US

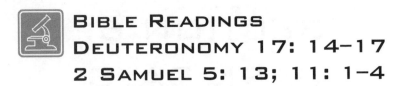

BIBLE READINGS
DEUTERONOMY 17: 14–17
2 SAMUEL 5: 13; 11: 1–4

DEUTERONOMY 17: 14–17

[14]When you enter the land the LORD your God is giving you and have taken possession of it and settled in it, and you say, "Let us set a king over us like all the nations around us," [15]be sure to appoint over you the king the LORD your God chooses. He must be from among your own brothers. Do not place a foreigner over you, one who is not a brother Israelite. [16]The king, moreover, must not acquire great numbers of horses for himself or make the people return to Egypt to get more of them, for the LORD has told you, "You are not to go back that way again." [17]He must not take many wives, or his heart will be led astray.

2 SAMUEL 5: 13

After he left Hebron, David took more concubines and wives in Jerusalem, and more sons and daughters were born to him.

2 SAMUEL 11: 1–4

In the spring, at the time when kings go off to war, David sent Joab out with the king's men and the whole Israelite army. They destroyed the Ammonites and besieged Rabbah. But David remained in Jerusalem. [2]One evening David got up from his bed and walked around on the roof of the palace. From the roof he saw a woman bathing. The woman was very beautiful, [3]and David sent someone to find out about her. The man said, "Isn't this Bathsheba, the daughter of Eliam and the wife of Uriah the Hittite?" [4]Then David sent messengers to get her.

THINK ABOUT IT DAY 29
THE FATAL WEAKNESS

There is no nice way to say this: David's fatal weakness was that he used women. God knows the weakness of human beings, and he warned the Israelites that kings would misuse their power and exploit the women in Israel.

David knew that passage in Deuteronomy and so did others who could have kept him true to God's commands. But David had ignored the Word of God and had misused his power to indulge his sexual desire.

Maybe he thought that sex would never get the better of him. But he was wrong. It was as if he'd taken a lion cub for a pet, thinking it would never turn on its master. But lion cubs grow up, and that night the lion turned and savaged David.

Young men, young women – you are no different from King David. Take a lion for a pet and one day it will turn on you and do you more harm than you can imagine.

One other point: there was no advance warning that temptation was coming his way. It might entangle you next week, or in twenty-three years time; Satan doesn't give you any warning. Keep pure: the best way to avoid getting bitten is not to take an untameable beast for a pet in the first place. No sex outside of marriage. God really does know best.

READ THIS THEN PRAY: How can a young man keep his way pure? By living according to your Word (Psalm 119: 9).

Prayer: Lord God, please keep my heart and body pure from sin. Give me your strength when I have to resist temptation. May I do my best to run away from sin when I find myself falling into it. Please direct me and make me willing to please you. In your name. Amen.

Who's Who: Ammonites; Bathsheba; Joab; Satan; Uriah
Words: Temptation
Maps and Place Names: Egypt; Hebron; Jerusalem; Rabbah

BIBLE READING
2 SAMUEL 11: 1–5

In the spring, at the time when kings go off to war, David sent Joab out with the king's men and the whole Israelite army. They destroyed the Ammonites and besieged Rabbah. But David remained in Jerusalem. [2]One evening David got up from his bed and walked around on the roof of the palace. From the roof he saw a woman bathing. The woman was very beautiful, [3]and David sent someone to find out about her. The man said, "Isn't this Bathsheba, the daughter of Eliam and the wife of Uriah the Hittite?" [4]Then David sent messengers to get her. She came to him, and he slept with her. (She had purified herself from her uncleanness.) Then she went back home. [5]The woman conceived and sent word to David, saying, "I am pregnant."

DUTY: David had duties as king so why wasn't he with his army? It is possible that if David had been performing his duty as a warrior and as king of his country he would not have fallen into temptation in the first place. As Christians we have duties – to read and study God's Word, to spend time in prayer, to attend the worship of God to be in fellowship with other Christians. These are good things for us to do. We need to do them for our spiritual health. We have other duties too such as doing our jobs; helping our families; school and studies etc. If we chose a life of idleness and sloth then we are going to find that it is easier for sin to creep in.

Boot Camp 003/Getting started with you

84

THINK ABOUT IT DAY 30
HOW NOT TO HANDLE
TEMPTATION – GIVE IN

Bathsheba wasn't wrong to have a bath. And you can't blame her for being beautiful – God made her beautiful! And she wasn't a loose-living woman who was anybody's for a laugh.

Neither was David looking for her – seeing her 'just happened'. There is a proverb which says, 'You can't stop birds flying round your head, but you can stop them making a nest in your hair.'

David should and could have said 'No' to himself. He could have reminded himself of the Word of God. He could have prayed for help. He could have run! He could have called a few friends over and asked them to pray with him. He could have gone out for a meal with them. He could have done a thousand things to resist.

But we often put more effort into resisting the common cold than we do into resisting the devil.

No one's pretending that it's easy to resist the tempter, but if David hadn't developed the habit of giving in to this kind of temptation at least he might have put up a fight.

Don't give the devil a foothold; don't try and resist him all on your own; don't forget that God is on your side in the battle; don't give in.

READ THIS THEN PRAY: ... God is faithful; he will not let you be tempted beyond what you can bear. But when you are tempted, he will also provide a way out so that you can stand up under it (1 Corinthians 10: 13).

Prayer: Lord God, when I feel tempted to sin, when I find that I desire to do what displeases you, help me to say no. You know where my weaknesses are and you have promised to help me defeat sin. When I feel too weak to tackle my temptations on my own help me to run straight to you for help. I pray this in your name. Amen.

Who's Who: Bathsheba; the devil; Hittite; Uriah;
Words: Faithful; Temptation; Tempter

BIBLE READING
2 SAMUEL 11: 6-17

[6]So David sent this word to Joab: "Send me Uriah the Hittite." And Joab sent him to David. [7]When Uriah came to him, David asked him how Joab was, how the soldiers were and how the war was going. [8]Then David said to Uriah, "Go down to your house and wash your feet." So Uriah left the palace, and a gift from the king was sent after him. [9]But Uriah slept at the entrance to the palace with all his master's servants and did not go down to his house. [10]When David was told, "Uriah did not go home," he asked him, "Haven't you just come from a distance? Why didn't you go home?" [11]Uriah said to David, "The ark and Israel and Judah are staying in tents, and my master Joab and my lord's men are camped in the open fields. How could I go to my house to eat and drink and lie with my wife? As surely as you live, I will not do such a thing!" [12]Then David said to him, "Stay here one more day, and tomorrow I will send you back." So Uriah remained in Jerusalem that day and the next. [13]At David's invitation, he ate and drank with him, and David made him drunk. But in the evening Uriah went out to sleep on his mat among his master's servants; he did not go home. [14]In the morning David wrote a letter to Joab and sent it with Uriah. [15]In it he wrote, "Put Uriah in the front line where the fighting is fiercest. Then withdraw from him so that he will be struck down and die." [16]So while Joab had the city under siege, he put Uriah at a place where he knew the strongest defenders were. [17]When the men of the city came out and fought against Joab, some of the men in David's army fell; moreover, Uriah the Hittite died.

Who's Who: Israel; Joab; Judah; Bathsheba; Uriah
Maps and Place Names: Jerusalem
Words: Ark; Compassion; Confess; Cross; Forgiveness; Repented

Boot Camp/005 Getting Started with Jesus Christ.

THINK ABOUT IT DAY 31
HOW NOT TO HANDLE SIN
– COVER UP

One sin leads to another unless we confess to God straightaway and ask his forgiveness.

David tried to cover the whole thing up. He tried to get Uriah to sleep with his wife so that it would look like the baby was his. But Uriah was a more honourable man than David and it didn't work.

So he misused his God-given power again to have Uriah killed by the enemy. It looked like it had worked this time.

But God sees everything. No one can hide sin from him.

The irony is that God has said that he will cover our sins. One of the key words for God dealing with sin is the word 'atonement'. It means to cover an offence so that it no longer comes between people.

David tried to cover up the sin with Bathsheba but if only he'd turned to God and repented, God would have covered his sin for him.

We all sin. We're all weak in some area or another of life. God, as we saw in Psalm 103, is full of compassion. He knows when we've fallen so there's no point covering it up. Jesus carried all our sins in his body on the cross. Tell him, say sorry, ask for his forgiveness and trust in Jesus' death on the cross. His blood will cover all your sin – forever!

READ THIS THEN PRAY: Blessed are they whose transgressions are forgiven, whose sins are covered (Romans 4: 7).

Prayer: Lord Jesus, thank you for covering my sins through the shedding of your blood on the cross. Turn my heart towards you so that I will bring my sins to you to be dealt with. I need forgiveness and I need you ... you alone. Amen.

BIBLE READING 2 SAMUEL 11: 26–27;12: 4–7

2 SAMUEL 11: 26–27

26When Uriah's wife heard that her husband was dead, she mourned for him. 27After the time of mourning was over, David had her brought to his house, and she became his wife and bore him a son. But the thing David had done displeased the LORD.

2 SAMUEL 12: 4–7

1The LORD sent Nathan to David. When he came to him, he said, "There were two men in a certain town, one rich and the other poor. 2The rich man had a very large number of sheep and cattle, 3but the poor man had nothing except one little ewe lamb that he had bought. He raised it, and it grew up with him and his children. It shared his food, drank from his cup and even slept in his arms. It was like a daughter to him. 4Now a traveller came to the rich man, but the rich man refrained from taking one of his own sheep or cattle to prepare a meal for the traveller who had come to him. Instead, he took the ewe lamb that belonged to the poor man and prepared it for the one who had come to him."
5David burned with anger against the man and said to Nathan, "As surely as the LORD lives, the man who did this deserves to die! 6He must pay for that lamb four times over, because he did such a thing and had no pity."
7Then Nathan said to David, "You are the man!"

Who's Who: Nathan; Uriah
Words: Conscience; Fellowship; Repentance; Sin

Boot Camp 003/Getting started with you
Boot Camp 004/Getting started with God

THINK ABOUT IT DAY 32
HOW NOT TO HANDLE GUILT
– DENY IT

God is deeply unhappy when we sin, and when, like David, we deny any guilt and try to live as if nothing had happened.

Which is what David had managed to do for maybe as long as a year. Every day people have watched as Bathsheba mourned then became another of David's wives, as the bump grew, as baby boy was born and nursed. Every day David lived as if nothing was wrong; no sin, no guilt, no shame: everything's fine. But it wasn't fine: David was living in denial of the truth.

The man who is supposed to rule in God's name and in obedience to his Word is living a guilty lie.

So through Nathan, God mercifully exposes the guilt and forces David to face it. It's no use pretending any more. It's the only way to restore true fellowship with God. And it's the only way to lift from David the baggage with which his denial has burdened him.

Is there something that you're trying to deny – as if it's never happened? Listen to your conscience. God can heal you more quickly from your sin than you can. In fact, we can't ever heal ourselves; we only make our hearts heavy and miserable. Repentance is the key to a joy-filled life.

READ THIS THEN PRAY: If we confess our sins, *God* is faithful and just and will forgive us our sins and purify us from all unrighteousness. If we claim we have not sinned, we make him out to be a liar and his Word has no place in our lives (1 John 1: 9–10).

Prayer: Lord God, I apologise for making you unhappy by sinning against you. Show me my sin. Help me to realise that I need to have you deal with it. Give me the courage to face up to what I have done wrong. Show me how pure you are so that I will turn away from my sin towards you. In your name I pray. Amen.

89

BIBLE READING
2 SAMUEL 12: 7-24

This is what the LORD, the God of Israel, says: `I anointed you king over Israel, and I delivered you from the hand of Saul. [8]I gave your master's house to you, and your master's wives into your arms. I gave you the house of Israel and Judah. And if all this had been too little, I would have given you even more. [9]Why did you despise the Word of the LORD by doing what is evil in his eyes? You struck down Uriah the Hittite with the sword and took his wife to be your own. You killed him with the sword of the Ammonites. [10]Now, therefore, the sword shall never depart from your house, because you despised me and took the wife of Uriah the Hittite to be your own.' [11]"This is what the LORD says: `Out of your own household I am going to bring calamity upon you. Before your very eyes I will take your wives and give them to one who is close to you, and he will lie with your wives in broad daylight. [12]You did it in secret, but I will do this thing in broad daylight before all Israel.'" [13]Then David said to Nathan, "I have sinned against the LORD." Nathan replied, "The LORD has taken away your sin. You are not going to die. [14]But because by doing this you have made the enemies of the LORD show utter contempt, the son born to you will die." [15]After Nathan had gone home, the LORD struck the child that Uriah's wife had borne to David, and he became ill. [16]David pleaded with God for the child. He fasted and went into his house and spent the nights lying on the ground. [17]The elders of his household stood beside him to get him up from the ground, but he refused, and he would not eat any food with them. [18]On the seventh day the child died. David's servants were afraid to tell him that the child was dead, for they thought, "While the child was still living, we spoke to David but he would not listen to us. How can we tell him the child is dead? He may do something desperate." [19]David noticed that his servants were whispering among themselves and he realised that the child was dead. "Is the child dead?" he asked. "Yes," they replied, "he is dead." [20]Then David got up from the ground. After he had washed, put on lotions and changed his clothes, he went into the house of the LORD and worshipped. Then he went to his own house, and at his request they served him food, and he ate. [21]His servants asked him, "Why are you acting in this way? While the child was alive, you fasted and wept, but now that the child is dead, you get up and eat!" [22]He answered, "While the child was still alive, I fasted and wept. I thought,'Who knows? The LORD may be gracious to me and let the child live.' [23]But now that he is dead, why should I fast? Can I bring him back again? I will go to him, but he will not return to me." [24]Then David comforted his wife, Bathsheba.

PROPHETS AND PROPHECY: There are many examples in God's Word of prophets who bring a message from the LORD. Here we see a prophet bringing a message to King David. He is warned that a great trouble will come on him from his own household. As you read on you will find out exactly how close this trouble was to David. You don't get much closer than your own child! David had sinned and he had thought that it was entirely his own secret. It is as though David has forgotten words that he wrote himself in Psalm 33: 'From heaven the LORD looks down and sees all mankind.'

MOURNING: It was a Bible time custom for mourners to wear sackcloth and pour ashes on their heads. This is why David would have needed to wash and put lotions on after his time of mourning was completed. But note that David's time of mourning doesn't start at the child's death – it ends then. This is because David knows that once the child is dead there is nothing more that can be done. His young son is now with the LORD God. David trusts his Heavenly Father and looks forward to the day when he will be with his God and with his child in heaven. This can give comfort to us when a loved one, who trusted in Jesus, has died. It is true that they will never return to this life – but if you and your loved one both trusted in the Lord Jesus Christ you can look forward to being together again in the future.

Who's Who: Ammonites; Bathsheba; Israel; Judah; Nathan; Saul; Uriah
Words: Anointed; Church; Fasted; Heaven

Boot Camp 003/Getting started with you
Boot Camp 004/Getting started with God

THINK ABOUT IT DAY 33
GOD WOUNDS AND HEALS

The punishment might seem very severe, though notice that David has the hope of seeing his son again in heaven and remember that he should never have had all the wives and concubines in the first place. But God is doing something here that he will often do in our lives. HE is wounding in order to heal.

A man in our church has recently had to lose part of his right leg. The surgeon had to wound him – even doing him permanent damage – in order to heal him. If he hadn't had that sever operation he would have been dead in a matter weeks from infection.

It's never nice at the time when God disciplines us. When he sends difficulties or trials that make life difficult, when he painfully puts his finger on a sin that we're trying to hide, it's not easy. But he disciplines us because he loves us, and he knows that if the sin is left unconfessed then the sin will turn into a habit, our consciences will become hard and the sin will spread like a deadly infection.

God might well wound us but only ever to heal us.

READ THIS THEN PRAY: *God* heals the broken hearted and binds up their wounds (Psalm 147: 3).

Prayer: Lord God, when you correct me and show me my sin make me thankful. I need to be directed in the right way. When difficult times come may these send me straight to you. Amen.

ZONE IN ON MAP

See full map of Israel on page 127 and
Place name index on pages 128–130
to find out more information on the following places:

Gibeon
Hebron and
Egypt

To find out more about these places look up the following
scripture verses:

Gibeon – Joshua 9; Joshua 10; 1 Kings 3:5; Nehemiah 3:7;
Jeremiah 41.

Hebron: Genesis 13:18; Genesis 23:19; Judges 1:20;
Judges 16:3

Egypt: Genesis 12:10; Genesis 37:28–36; Genesis 41:41;
Exodus 1:8–14; Leviticus 11:45; Matthew 2:13;
Hebrews 11:26–29.

BIBLE READINGS
2 CORINTHIANS 5: 21
1 PETER 2: 21–25
1 JOHN 3: 5

2 CORINTHIANS 5: 21

God made him who had no sin to be sin for us, so that in him we might become the righteousness of God.

1 PETER 2: 21–25

Christ suffered for you, leaving you an example, that you should follow in his steps. 22"He committed no sin, and no deceit was found in his mouth." 23When they hurled their insults at him, he did not retaliate; when he suffered, he made no threats. Instead, he entrusted himself to him who judges justly. 24He himself bore our sins in his body on the tree, so that we might die to sins and live for righteousness; by his wounds you have been healed. 25For you were like sheep going astray, but now you have returned to the Shepherd and Overseer of your souls.

1 JOHN 3: 5

You know that he appeared so that he might take away our sins. And in him is no sin.

TREE: This is a word that is sometimes used to describe the cross on which Jesus died. In Deuteronomy 21: 23 it mentions that anyone who is hung on a tree is under God's curse. This is what happened to Jesus when he took the punishment of his people. He didn't deserve this – we did. But Jesus was cursed by God so that his people wouldn't have to be.

Who's Who: John; Peter
Maps and Place Names: Corinth

Boot Camp 004/Getting started with God

THINK ABOUT IT DAY 34
JESUS IS PURE

Here's the wonderful thing: Jesus was totally pure for you and for me. Jesus was the kind of person that God wants us all to be, but knowing that not even one of us is like that, he sent his son to be that for us – on our behalf. Jesus is pure for you so that you can trust his purity. We thought about that when we looked at Psalm 24.

And because Jesus was totally, 100% without sin in every part of his life he didn't have his own sins to bear on the cross. He could take ours away because he had no baggage of his own. Because he never once offended the Father he could take our offences on the cross.

There on Calvary an enormous swap took place. All our sin was laid on him, and all his righteousness was made ours. In him we become clean: no stains, no nasty marks, no dirty patches. Trusting in Jesus means that our filthy rags can be swapped for royal robes that are totally clean. It's a new life, a new start.

Have you asked to be made clean in Jesus? Have you asked God for a new start yet? If you haven't, ask now. He will hear and answer you.

READ THIS THEN PRAY: Therefore, if anyone is in Christ, he is a new creation; the old has gone, the new has come (2 Corinthians 5: 17).

Prayer: Lord Jesus, thank you for exchanging the sin of your people and giving in its place your own righteousness. Sin only destroys, your righteousness saves. Give me the desire in my heart for a brand new start. Take me away from walking towards sin and head me in the right direction - towards you and your Word. Amen.

BIBLE READING
PSALM 51

For the director of music. A psalm of David. When the prophet Nathan came to him after David had committed adultery with Bathsheba.

Have mercy on me, O God, according to your unfailing love; according to your great compassion blot out my transgressions. ²Wash away all my iniquity and cleanse me from my sin. ³For I know my transgressions, and my sin is always before me. ⁴Against you, you only, have I sinned and done what is evil in your sight, so that you are proved right when you speak and justified when you judge. ⁵Surely I was sinful at birth, sinful from the time my mother conceived me. ⁶Surely you desire truth in the inner parts; you teach me wisdom in the inmost place. ⁷Cleanse me with hyssop, and I shall be clean; wash me, and I shall be whiter than snow. ⁸Let me hear joy and gladness; let the bones you have crushed rejoice. ⁹Hide your face from my sins and blot out all my iniquity. ¹⁰Create in me a pure heart, O God, and renew a steadfast spirit within me. ¹¹Do not cast me from your presence or take your Holy Spirit from me. ¹²Restore to me the joy of your salvation and grant me a willing spirit, to sustain me. ¹³Then I will teach transgressors your ways, and sinners will turn back to you. ¹⁴Save me from bloodguilt, O God, the God who saves me, and my tongue will sing of your righteousness. ¹⁵O Lord, open my lips, and my mouth will declare your praise. ¹⁶You do not delight in sacrifice, or I would bring it; you do not take pleasure in burnt offerings. ¹⁷The sacrifices of God are a broken spirit; a broken and contrite heart, O God, you will not despise. ¹⁸In your good pleasure make Zion prosper; build up the walls of Jerusalem. ¹⁹Then there will be righteous sacrifices, whole burnt offerings to delight you; then bulls will be offered on your altar.

Who's Who: Bathsheba; Nathan

Words: Adultery; Altar; Believe; Bloodguilt; Burnt offerings; Compassion; Contrite; Forgiveness; Holiness; Hyssop; Iniquity; Penitance; Repent; Righteousness; Sacrifice; Sin; Sinners; Sustain; Transgressions; Transgressors

THINK ABOUT IT DAY 35 WHAT GOD DESIRES FROM US

It took long enough but by God's mercy David was brought to the point where he did repent and seek forgiveness. Out of the disaster came this Psalm of penitence which God has used to help countless thousands of Christians get right with God again after falling to temptation. It's certainly been an enormous help to me.

What's the thing that God wants from you most? Is it that you should be rich, or clever, or good-looking or famous or have a great figure or be very popular? Is it that you should grind yourself down doing good things for everyone or making other huge sacrifices in your life?

No.

What God wants from you most is that you come to him when you're broken and deeply, deeply sorry about your sin. He won't despise you, he loves you. He wants you to have a heart that's as sensitive to the awfulness of sin and the beauty of holiness as his heart is.

So don't spend you life trying to be good on the outside while your heart gets harder and harder. Ask God to give you a heart that's tender towards him because it's full of love for him.

READ THIS THEN PRAY: Without faith it is impossible to please God, because anyone who comes to him must believe that he exists and that he rewards those who earnestly seek him (Hebrews 11: 6).

Prayer: Lord God, I know that I must please you and to do that I must have faith. I ask that you give me a faith in you - so that I can believe in you and trust in you. You are the only one who can give this amazing gift to me – real faith comes from no one else. I ask this in your name. Amen.

SECTION 7: PAIN AND PRAISE

DAY 36: 2 SAMUEL 15: 1–12

THE KINGDOM IS SHAKEN

DAY 37: 2 SAMUEL 15: 13–26

DAVID FLEES FROM DANGER

DAY 38: 2 SAMUEL 19: 9–23

RETURNING TO REIGN

DAY 39: 2 SAMUEL 22: 44–23:7

GOD IS MY ROCK

DAY 40: ISAIAH 9: 6–7 &

HEBREWS 1: 1–9

JESUS IS KING FOR EVER

BIBLE READING
2 SAMUEL 15: 1-12

In the course of time, Absalom provided himself with a chariot and horses and with fifty men to run ahead of him. [2]He would get up early and stand by the side of the road leading to the city gate. Whenever anyone came with a complaint to be placed before the king for a decision, Absalom would call out to him, "What town are you from?" He would answer, "Your servant is from one of the tribes of Israel." [3]Then Absalom would say to him, "Look, your claims are valid and proper, but there is no representative of the king to hear you." [4]And Absalom would add, "If only I were appointed judge in the land! Then everyone who has a complaint or case could come to me and I would see that he receives justice." [5]Also, whenever anyone approached him to bow down before him, Absalom would reach out his hand, take hold of him and kiss him. [6]Absalom behaved in this way towards all the Israelites who came to the king asking for justice, and so he stole the hearts of the men of Israel. [7]At the end of four years, Absalom said to the king, "Let me go to Hebron and fulfil a vow I made to the LORD. [8]While your servant was living at Geshur in Aram, I made this vow: 'If the LORD takes me back to Jerusalem, I will worship the LORD in Hebron.'" [9]The king said to him, "Go in peace." So he went to Hebron. [10]Then Absalom sent secret messengers throughout the tribes of Israel to say, "As soon as you hear the sound of the trumpets, then say, 'Absalom is king in Hebron.'" [11]Two hundred men from Jerusalem had accompanied Absalom. They had been invited as guests and went quite innocently, knowing nothing about the matter. [12]While Absalom was offering sacrifices, he also sent for Ahithophel the Gilonite, David's counsellor, to come from Giloh, his home town. And so the conspiracy gained strength, and Absalom's following kept on increasing.

Who's Who: Absalom; Ahithophel; Gilonite
Words: Faithful; Judgement
Maps and Place Names: Aram; Geshur; Giloh; Hebron; Jerusalem

THINK ABOUT IT DAY 36
THE KINGDOM IS SHAKEN

The shockwaves of David's sin and of God's judgement shook the unity of the kingdom. A kind of civil war broke out between David's sons in which Absalom killed many of his brothers. The plan was simple: get rid of the other heirs to the throne, then get rid of Dad. Absalom used his natural abilities to feed his own hunger for power. He had no thoughts towards God at all.

He craftily wins over the hearts of the people, then under the cloak of a lie he has himself proclaimed king in Hebron. He had patiently waited until the time was right, then his greed explodes upon clueless David.

As David gets older he suffers deep opposition from his own closest company. Even the son that he loves betrays him. The only thing in life that he can be certain of is that God will be with him. Jealousy, connected to cleverness and greed, can ruin relationships and can de-rail the best of our work. And keeping faithful to Jesus doesn't always mean that life gets easier.

Behind Absalom is the devil who will always try to exploit sinfulness. No wonder Jesus told his disciples to be on their guard.

READ THIS THEN PRAY: Let us hold unswervingly to the hope we profess, for he who promised is faithful (Hebrews 10: 23).

Prayer: Thank you, God, that you will always be with your people. Make me one of your family. The truth in your Word is utterly trustworthy because you are trustworthy. You give your people hope – and this is not a false hope – it a true and definite hope. Thank you for this. Amen.

BIBLE READING
2 SAMUEL 15: 13–26

[13]A messenger came and told David, "The hearts of the men of Israel are with Absalom." [14]Then David said to all his officials who were with him in Jerusalem, "Come! We must flee, or none of us will escape from Absalom. We must leave immediately, or he will move quickly to overtake us and bring ruin upon us and put the city to the sword." [15]The king's officials answered him, "Your servants are ready to do whatever our lord the king chooses." [16]The king set out, with his entire household following him; but he left ten concubines to take care of the palace. [17]So the king set out, with all the people following him, and they halted at a place some distance away. [18]All his men marched past him, along with all the Kerethites and Pelethites; and all the six hundred Gittites who had accompanied him from Gath marched before the king. [19]The king said to Ittai the Gittite, "Why should you come along with us? Go back and stay with King Absalom. You are a foreigner, an exile from your homeland. [20]You came only yesterday. And today shall I make you wander about with us, when I do not know where I am going? Go back, and take your countrymen. May kindness and faithfulness be with you." [21]But Ittai replied to the king, "As surely as the LORD lives, and as my lord the king lives, wherever my lord the king may be, whether it means life or death, there will your servant be." [22]David said to Ittai, "Go ahead, march on." So Ittai the Gittite marched on with all his men and the families that were with him. [23]The whole countryside wept aloud as all the people passed by. The king also crossed the Kidron Valley, and all the people moved on towards the desert. [24]Zadok was there, too, and all the Levites who were with him were carrying the ark of the covenant of God. They set down the ark of God, and Abiathar offered sacrifices until all the people had finished leaving the city. [25]Then the king said to Zadok, "Take the ark of God back into the city. If I find favour in the LORD's eyes, he will bring me back and let me see it and his dwelling-place again. [26]But if he says, `I am not pleased with you,' then I am ready; let him do to me whatever seems good to him."

THINK ABOUT IT DAY 37
DAVID FLEES FROM DANGER

This is a tragic scene: the people there wept at the awfulness of what was happening. But there are three bright stars in this dark night.

First, David isn't a coward. In fact he's showing amazing self-sacrificial concern for his people in Jerusalem. He knows that if he stays there's the very real possibility of a blood-bath in the city, with many innocent people being killed. He flees for their sake.

Second, Ittai shows great kindness and loyalty to David because he has a sense of God's hand on David. Such friendship in distressing times gives huge encouragement.

Third, David has quiet, complete trust in whatever God is doing. He is content to let God's will be done and to accept whatever he sends without doubting his love or his wisdom. So he has peace in the middle of the earthquake that is rocking his kingdom.

Put others first, even when it costs you; be a true and good friend because of Jesus and gladly appreciate such friendship when it's shown to you; find peace by accepting from God's hand whatever he sends. Then even the tragedies that might strike you will turn out for good.

READ THIS THEN PRAY: "Father, if you are willing, take this cup from me; yet not my will, but yours be done." (Luke 22: 42).

Prayer: Lord Jesus, you understood what would happen at the cross yet you were willing for it to go ahead. You wanted to obey your Father above everything. It is your selfless act that gives sinners salvation. Help me to realise that I am one who needs that saving help. Show me how to be selfless by putting others before myself and God first of all. Amen.

Who's Who: Absalom; Gittite; Ittai; Levites; Zadok
Words: Ark of the covenant of God
Maps and Place Names: Jerusalem; Kidron Valley

103

BIBLE READINGS
2 SAMUEL 19: 9–23;
20: 3

2 SAMUEL 19: 9–23

[9]Throughout the tribes of Israel, the people were all arguing with each other, saying, "The king delivered us from the hand of our enemies; he is the one who rescued us from the hand of the Philistines. But now he has fled the country because of Absalom; [10]and Absalom, whom we anointed to rule over us, has died in battle. So why do you say nothing about bringing the king back?" [11]King David sent this message to Zadok and Abiathar, the priests: "Ask the elders of Judah, `Why should you be the last to bring the king back to his palace, since what is being said throughout Israel has reached the king at his quarters? [12]You are my brothers, my own flesh and blood. So why should you be the last to bring back the king?' [13]And say to Amasa, `Are you not my own flesh and blood? May God deal with me, be it ever so severely, if from now on you are not the commander of my army in place of Joab.'" [14]He won over the hearts of all the men of Judah as though they were one man. They sent word to the king, "Return, you and all your men." [15]Then the king returned and went as far as the Jordan. Now the men of Judah had come to Gilgal to go out and meet the king and bring him across the Jordan. [16]Shimei, son of Gera, the Benjamite from Bahurim, hurried down with the men of Judah to meet King David. [17]With him were a thousand Benjamites, along with Ziba, the steward of Saul's household, and his fifteen sons and twenty servants. They rushed to the Jordan, where the king was. [18]They crossed at the ford to take the king's household over and to do whatever he wished. When Shimei, son of Gera, crossed the Jordan, he fell prostrate before the king [19]and said to him, "May my lord not hold me guilty. Do not remember how your servant did wrong on the day my lord the king left Jerusalem. May the king put it out of his mind. [20]For I your servant know that I have sinned, but today I have come here as the first of the whole house of Joseph to come down and meet my lord the king." [21]Then Abishai, son of Zeruiah said, "Shouldn't Shimei be put to death for this? He cursed the LORD's anointed." [22]David replied, "What do you and I have in common, you sons of Zeruiah? This day you

have become my adversaries! Should anyone be put to death in Israel today? Do I not know that today I am king over Israel?" [23]So the king said to Shimei, "You shall not die." And the king promised him on oath.

2 SAMUEL 20: 3

When David returned to his palace in Jerusalem, he took the ten concubines he had left to take care of the palace and put them in a house under guard. He provided for them, but did not lie with them. They were kept in confinement till the day of their death, living as widows.

 Who's Who: Abiathar; Abishai son of Zeruiah; Absalom; Amasa; Benjamites; Joab; Judah; Philistines; Satan; Shimei son of Gera; Zadok; Ziba
Words: Concubines; Forgiven; Oath
Maps and Place Names: Bahurim; Gilgal; Jerusalem; Jordan

THINK ABOUT IT DAY 38
RETURNING TO REIGN

You'd think that when God gives David victory over Absalom and clears the way for his return to Jerusalem, there would be singing, feasting, and dancing in the streets.

Instead, David's return is quiet. The sense of triumph is quietened by grief at Absalom's death, but it's also a gentler, kinder, more spiritually mature David who returns. He could have had Shimei beheaded on the spot. Shimei had pelted David with rocks when he was fleeing Jerusalem and had hurled curses on him as well. But David is returning to rule in God's way, so the God who has been gracious and forgiving to David is the example of how he should be to Shimei. David has no place in his heart or his kingdom for merciless vengeance.

Then, when he actually arrives back at his palace, he turns away from the concubines that once he had enjoyed. Those sins now hold no attraction for him. God has made David wiser and better through the terrible events that Absalom's mad pride had triggered. Satan must have thought he had won against God's King, but God won. The godliness that David showed in the later years proved it.

As God has been to us, so we must be to others. Godliness with contentment is great gain; we show it by forgiving others as we have been forgiven.

READ THIS THEN PRAY: And when you stand praying, if you hold anything against anyone, forgive him, so that your Father in heaven may forgive you your sins (Mark 11: 25).

Prayer: Lord Jesus, before I come to you in prayer show me my heart and teach me if I am holding any grudges – against you or against others. Because you forgive those who ask sincerely to be saved from their sins, help me to forgive those who ask me for the same. In your name. Amen.

ZONE IN ON MAP

See full map of Israel on page 127 and
Place name index on pages 128–130
to find out more information on the following places:

Gilgal
Jordan
Corinth

To find out more about these places look up the following
scripture verses:

Gilgal – Deuteronomy 11:30; Joshua 4:19–20; Joshua 5:9–10;
2 Kings 2:1; 2 Kings 4:38

Jordan – Genesis 13: 10–11; Genesis 50: 10–11;
Deuteronomy 3: 27; Deuteronomy 27: 2; Joshua 3: 13–17; 2
Kings 5: 10; Matthew 3: 5–7; Matthew 3: 13; Matthew 4: 15

Corinth: Acts 18: 1; Acts 18: 8; 2 Corinthians 1: 1;
2 Timothy 4: 20

BIBLE READING:
2 SAMUEL 22: 44-51;
23: 1-7

2 SAMUEL 22: 44-51

44"You have delivered me from the attacks of my people; you have preserved me as the head of nations. People I did not know are subject to me, 45and foreigners come cringing to me; as soon as they hear me, they obey me. 46They all lose heart; they come trembling from their strongholds. 47"The LORD lives! Praise be to my Rock! Exalted be God, the Rock, my Saviour! 48He is the God who avenges me, who puts the nations under me, 49who sets me free from my enemies. You exalted me above my foes; from violent men you rescued me. 50Therefore I will praise you, O LORD, among the nations; I will sing praises to your name. 51He gives his king great victories; he shows unfailing kindness to his anointed, to David and his descendants for ever."

2 SAMUEL 23: 1-7

1These are the last words of David: "The oracle of David son of Jesse, the oracle of the man exalted by the Most High, the man anointed by the God of Jacob, Israel's singer of songs: 2"The Spirit of the LORD spoke through me; his Word was on my tongue. 3The God of Israel spoke, the Rock of Israel said to me: `When one rules over men in righteousness, when he rules in the fear of God, 4he is like the light of morning at sunrise on a cloudless morning, like the brightness after rain that brings the grass from the earth.' 5"Is not my house right with God? Has he not made with me an everlasting covenant, arranged and secured in every part? Will he not bring to fruition my salvation and grant me my every desire? 6But evil men are all to be cast aside like thorns, which are not gathered with the hand. 7Whoever touches thorns uses a tool of iron or the shaft of a spear; they are burned up where they lie."

Words: Anointed; Covenant; Exalted; Faithful; Oracle; Praise; Righteousness; Salvation; Subject

THINK ABOUT IT DAY 39
GOD IS MY ROCK

What an up and down life David had. Great and golden times but terrible ones as well. Trustworthy and loyal friends but also those who turned out to be dangerous, thorny characters. Deep faith and courageous obedience but also spiritual weakness and compromise. In all the changing scenes of his life, one person has been as steady and reliable as a rock. God has been a secure foundation for David: always there for him; always true, always loving and always faithful to his promises.

Your life will go through many changes, some good, some very painful. You will learn difficult lessons about other people and almost certainly about yourself. The same God that David looked up to and prayed to, who showed David rock-like love, is here for you.

Will you build your life on the security that God alone can give you? You will find no one in life as reliable and faithful as God; no matter how awful life gets you can always trust his love for you. Jesus trusted the Father's love even on the cross. You can trust him too.

"The LORD lives! Praise be to my Rock! Exalted be God, the Rock, my Saviour!" (1 Samuel 22: 47)

You too can praise God for being your Rock, your Saviour. You can do it until your dying day.

READ THIS THEN PRAY: God's solid foundation stands firm, sealed with this inscription: "The Lord knows those who are his," and, "Everyone who confesses the name of the Lord must turn away from wickedness." (2 Timothy 2: 19).

Prayer: Lord Jesus, you are faithful, true and strong. If I build my life on any other thing then it will be weak and useless. Help me to build my life on you and your truth. Amen.

Boot Camp 004/Getting started with God

BIBLE READINGS
ISAIAH 9: 6-7 &
HEBREWS 1: 1-9

ISAIAH 9: 6-7

For to us a child is born, to us a son is given, and the government will be on his shoulders. And he will be called Wonderful Counsellor, Mighty God, Everlasting Father, Prince of Peace. [7]Of the increase of his government and peace there will be no end. He will reign on David's throne and over his kingdom, establishing and upholding it with justice and righteousness from that time on and for ever. The zeal of the LORD Almighty will accomplish this.

HEBREWS 1: 1-9

In the past God spoke to our forefathers through the prophets at many times and in various ways, [2]but in these last days he has spoken to us by his Son, whom he appointed heir of all things, and through whom he made the universe. [3]The Son is the radiance of God's glory and the exact representation of his being, sustaining all things by his powerful Word. After he had provided purification for sins, he sat down at the right hand of the Majesty in heaven. [4]So he became as much superior to the angels as the name he has inherited is superior to theirs. [5]For to which of the angels did God ever say, "You are my Son; today I have become your Father"? Or again, "I will be his Father, and he will be my Son"? [6]And again, when God brings his firstborn into the world, he says, "Let all God's angels worship him." [7]In speaking of the angels he says, "He makes his angels winds, his servants flames of fire." [8]But about the Son he says, "Your throne, O God, will last for ever and ever, and righteousness will be the sceptre of your kingdom. [9]You have loved righteousness and hated wickedness; therefore God, your God, has set you above your companions by anointing you with the oil of joy."

Words: Angels; Anointing; Compassion; Covenant; Established; Eternity; Heaven; Holiness; Infinitely; Judgement; Prophets; Purification; Righteousness; Sceptre

THINK ABOUT IT DAY 40
JESUS IS KING FOR EVER

As we saw earlier, the one who would fulfil the amazing promise of God to David is Jesus. Not in David's day, but through the one born in David's line, God's promise has been kept, for Jesus is King for ever.

If David at his best was a good king, Jesus is infinitely better. If David ruled with a degree of kindness, Jesus is infinitely kind. If David ruled with bright flashes of purity, Jesus is eternally radiant with purity. If David showed compassion on occasions, Jesus never ceases to regard you with compassion. If David protected his people at cost to himself, Jesus has laid down his life to save you from death and judgement. Everything about David that made people's spirits lift for a while only hinted at the one who would raise people from death for ever.

David's earthly throne is gone. But Jesus, his matchless and glorious successor, has a throne that will never disappear into history.

Jesus, King for ever, calls you to live as one of his royal companions, to share his home and to live in the light of his glory for all eternity. Unending fellowship with the King of heaven is what he holds out to you. Don't be like those who turned against King David in his lifetime or those who still turn away from great David's greater son. If you haven't done this already in your life, ask him to reign in your life as the King who saves for ever. Ask him now.

READ THIS THEN PRAY: ...I will not lie to David – that his line will continue for ever and his throne endure before me like the sun; it will be established for ever like the moon, the faithful witness in the sky" (Psalm 89: 34–37).

Prayer: Lord Jesus, may you reign in my life, as my King forever. Change my heart from being one that seeks my own gain to one that longs for you. Amen.

Boot Camp 004/Getting started with God
Boot Camp 005/Getting started with Jesus

RESEARCH FACILITY

WHO'S WHO: Get introduced to the main characters. Pages 114–117.

WORDS: Root out the meanings of certain words. Pages 118–125.

MAPS and PLACE NAMES: Find out about the places in the stories. See for yourself where it all happened. Pages 126–130.#

WHO'S WHO

DAVID AND HIS FAMILY

Jesse: The father of David and his brothers, which included Eliab, Abinadab and Shammah.

David: The shepherd boy who was anointed by Samuel to replace Saul as king. Because of this David refers to himself and on occasions to Saul as the Lord's anointed. From a young age he trusted God. He wrote many songs in the book of Psalms which is why he is referred to as Israel's Singer of Songs or the Psalmist. He is in Jesus' family tree so that is why Jesus is also known as Great David's greater son. He defeated the giant Goliath and went on to be a great King. Though a godly man he made mistakes but repented of them.

Abigail: She was a wise woman married to a foolish man called Nabal. Her wisdom was used to protect her household and King David. After Nabal's death Abigail became one of David's wives.

Absalom: One of King David's sons, who masterminded a rebellion against his father, but who was killed by David's soldiers.

Solomon: One of King David's sons, and the heir to the throne.

Bathsheba: She was the wife of Uriah, an honourable man. Bathsheba had an affair with King David. David organised the death of her husband in order to try and cover up their sin of adultary. She later became his wife and was Solomon's mother.

SAUL AND HIS HOUSEHOLD

Saul: The first king of Israel who failed to follow God's law. He lost his throne and died in battle by falling on his own sword.

Jonathan: Saul's son and heir. He recognized David as the Lord's anointed and was a good and faithful friend to him. He dies in battle alongside his father.

Mephibosheth: Jonathan's son. He was crippled in an accident when he was five years old. The news of his father and his grandfather's death had reached his home so his nurse ran to escape with the child and dropped him, causing his injuries.

Ziba: A servant of Saul. David asked him if any of Saul's family survived. Ziba told him of 'the cripple Mephibosheth', Jonathan's son.

TRIBES, KINGS AND ENEMIES

Arameans: They allied themselves with Hadadezer to fight against David and were defeated.

Benjamites: A Hebrew tribe. Descendants of Jacob's son – Benjamin.

Edomites: Descendants of Esau. David defeated them at the Valley of Salt.

Gilonite: A resident of the town of Giloh.

Gittites: This foreign tribe appear to have joined forces with David. Two notable Gittites were Obed-Edom, whose house the ark of the Lord remained in for a while, and Ittai who insisted on remaining with David instead of going back to Jerusalem and Absalom.

Goliath: The giant warrior of the Philistine tribe who was over nine feet tall but was defeated by David.

Hadadezer: At the Euphrates river Hadadezer's entire army was defeated by David.

Hiram King of Tyre: He was instrumental in building a palace for David out of cedar logs.

Hittites: Long before David's day they allowed Abraham to bury his wife, Sarah, in a cave that he purchased from them. They were not Israelites. Uriah was a Hittite showing us that people from this tribe joined forces with David.

Jebusites: They originally lived in Jerusalem before David conquered them.

Kerethites and Pelethites: Two associated tribes often mentioned together. Both appear to have been part of David's mercenary army and not part of the main Israelite army. They had a different commander: Benaiah.

Levites: A Hebrew tribe. The Levites were given the responsibility of the priesthood and looking after God's house and the sacrifices.

Israelites: Israel was the name given by God to Jacob. Thus his descendants are called people of Israel or Israelites.

Moabites: David's great-grandmother Ruth was a Moabite. David also deafeated this tribe.

Philistines: The tribe to which Goliath belonged. Anotorious enemy of the Israelite people. Many battles were fought between the Israelites and the Philistines.

Tou king of Hamath: He was at war with Hadadezer. When he heard of David's victory over Hadadezer he sent his son with gifts and congratulations.

Ziphites: They betrayed David to King Saul.

OTHERS CHARACTERS FROM THE STORY OF DAVID

Abiathar: He was a priest in Israel along with Zadok.

Abner: The commander of Saul's army. He was the son of Ner,

Saul's uncle. Abner was responsible for the death of the young man, Asahel, (Joab and Abishai's brother) during combat.

Ahithophel: He was a Gilonite and counsellor of David. He joined forces with David's rebel son, Absalom.

Amasa: He was chosen by David to replace Joab as commander in chief of the army after Joab's involvement with the death of Absalom. He was eventually murdered by Joab.

Ammiel: Father of Bathsheeba, David's wife.

Asahel: One of David's young fighters. He pursued Abner who was a much more experienced warrior. Abner tried to persuade Asahel to give up but he would not so the young man was killed by Abner during the ensuing combat.

Ittai: He was a Gittite and a foreigner who supported King David at the time of Absalom's rebellion.

Joab: Joab was one of David's men and the brother of Asahel. He avenged his brother's death by killing Abner. David instructed Joab to show repentance by walking in front of Abner's funeral procession in sackcloth and ashes.

Makir: Son of Ammiel in Lo Debar - Mephibosheth stayed with him for a while.

Nabal: Abigail's first husband.

Nathan: He was a prophet of the Lord God in Israel. He was the one sent by God to speak to David after he committed adultery with Bathsheba.

Samuel: He was dedicated to serve in the tabernacle of God from a very early age. As a young child God spoke directly to him. Later he was God's prophet and spokesperson to the people of Israel and anointed both King Saul and King David.

Shimei: He threw rocks and curses at David as he left Jerusalem to escape Absalom. He pled for mercy when David was finally victorious.

Uriah: The husband of Bathsheba with whom David committed adultery. He was a Hittite and was one of David's military men.

Uzzah: He and his brother carried the ark of the Lord. Uzzah was struck down dead by God when he tried to stop the ark falling over.

Zadok: He was a priest in Israel along with Abiathar.

Zeruiah: The mother of Joab and Abishai

OTHER OLD TESTAMENT CHARACTERS

Abraham: God chose Abraham to be the father of the Jewish nation. God made a promise to him that his descendants would have a land of their own one day.

Caleb: One of the spies who entered the Promised Land and came back with a good report.
Isaac: The son of Abraham.
Isaiah: The writer of the book of Isaiah in the Old Testament. He was a prophet and was given future revelations about the coming of the Lord Jesus Christ.
Jacob: The son of Isaac.
Joshua: One of the spies who entered the Promised Land and came back with a good report. He went on to lead the Israelites after Moses' death.
Judah: The fourth son of Jacob by Leah.
Moses: He was born to a Hebrew family when the Hebrews were Egyptian slaves. Moses was kept safe and was eventually taken under the wing of Pharaoh's own daughter. He went on to lead the Hebrews out of Egypt to the land that God had promised.
Tempter: See devil/Satan below.

NEW TESTAMENT CHARACTERS
Satan/the devil: A fallen angel. He first tempted Adam and Eve in the Garden of Eden.
Jesus: The Son of God, Saviour. Born in Bethlehem, crucified at Calvary and raised to life on the third day.
John: One of Jesus' disciples and the writer of the Gospel of John.
Joseph and Mary: Mary was the mother of the Lord Jesus. She was betrothed to Joseph who knew that the child in her was conceived by the power of the Holy Spirit. He agreed to marry her and did not know her in a sexual way until after their marriage.
Luke: Writer of the Gospel of Luke and the Book of Acts. A doctor and a travelling companion of Paul.
Matthew: Writer of the Gospel of Matthew. A tax collector who became one of Jesus' disciples. He was also called Levi.
Paul: An Apostle who wrote many New Testament epistles.
Peter: One of the disciples of Jesus and a writer of two books in the New Testament.

WORDS

adultery: An adulterer sins against their wife or husband by chosing to treat another person as their wife or husband. They disobey God's commandment, 'You shall not commit adultery.'

adversity: Very difficult circumstances.

altar: A structure on which sacrifices and offerings were made to God in the temple. Other religions had altars on which they made offerings to false gods.

angels/heavenly Hosts: Heavenly beings created by God to be his messengers and servants.

anointed; anointing: To be anointed is when something, usually oil, is smeared or rubbed onto you. At times this act of anointing signifies that the anointed person is being set aside for a special office. Kings are anointed at coronations to show that they have authority to rule. It is an outward sign that they are the king. Jesus is God's anointed. He has the authority to rule all.

ark/the ark of God/the ark of the covenant of God: This was the gold covered chest that lay in the Most Holy Place in the temple.

balsam: A resin obtained from trees or plants, containing essential oils such as benzoic and cinnamic acid. It is aromatic and can be used for healing and soothing as well as for anointing.

believe; believers: To believe means to know God, not just know about him, but actually know him as your personal saviour. If you do then you are a believer in the Lord Jesus Christ.

besiege: This is what an enemy army does to a city that it is attacking. It surrounds the city and does not let anything in or out of it.

bier: A stand or structure on which a corpse was laid before burial, and was then carried on to the graveside.

bless: When God gives undeserved favour and kindness and when people, including us, do the same for others.

bloodguilt: This is guilt incurred through bloodshed of innocent victims. Killing in self defence was exempt from this.

burnt offerings: These offerings were completely burnt on the altar as a sign of total dedication to God. The smoke ascended heavenwards to symbolise that the offering was being made to God.

church: A building where people gather together to worship God. It is also the group of people who follow Jesus. The church of

Christ is in many countries around the world. It is growing every day.

compassion: A feeling of distress for the unhappy circumstances of others; a merciful love that shows care for others.

concubines: They were female servants that a king or master would have sexual relations with. This was against God's law. Though an accepted practice in some societies.

confess: To admit to doing something wrong. We can confess our sins to God and he is faithful and just and will forgive us our sins.

conscience: This is the inner conviction or urging that enables you to do good and to distinguish between right and wrong.

consecrate: This is when you devote something or someone to God's service.

contrite: Very sorry.

covenant: This is God's promise to the Israelites and their commitment to worship him alone. It is a solemn and binding agreement between God and his people in which he makes promises and requires certain behaviour from them.

cross: In the New Testament it was an instrument of punishment for criminals. Jesus died on a cross, to take our punishment for sin.

cut off: Destroyed; killed.

established: Created or set up.

eternal/eternity: Eternal means never having had a beginning and never having an end. This is what God is like. He is eternal. We are created by God so we aren't eternal like he is. Our lives in this world are limited by time. God created time for us. We had a beginning when we were conceived and though our lives here will end when we die our souls will exist forever. Eternity has no limits. It had no beginning and it will have no end. It is infinite. This is impossible for us to fully understand but the Bible teaches us that when we die we too will be in eternity. Our souls and resurrected bodies will live eternally in heaven or die eternally in hell. These are solemn thoughts but it is amazing that when we trust completely in what the Lord Jesus Christ has done and understand who he is we can look forward to enjoying eternity with God in heaven for ever.

exalted: Praised highly or promoted.

faith and faithful: Faith is a word used to describe believing in God and Jesus Christ. The Bible describes faith as being certain of what you do not see. Though we can't see God we know he is real, we know his Word is true and faithful and that we can trust in the Lord Jesus Christ to save us from sin. This is faith. The word faithful used to describe God, means completely trustworthy. We can always rely on him to do the right thing, the just thing. He is perfect and holy. We can depend on him. He is faithful. We can learn from his example.

false witnesses: Liars

father: A title used to address God in prayer because of our relationship to him.

fasted/fast: To fast is when someone abstains from food and drink in order to concentrate on God's Word and prayer.

fellowship: Companionship and friendship.

fellowship offering: This is also referred to as a peace offering. An animal without spot or blemish was sacrificed to God in order to procure peace between God and the sinners who were making the offering. Read about this in Leviticus chapter 3.

forgive,/forgiven/forgiveness: When we are forgiven God looks on our sin and no longer holds us accountable for them or deserving of punishment. He accepts us into his family because of Christ's death on the cross.

forsake: To abandon someone.

garrison: Soldiers who guard a fort; the fort itself or to station soldiers in a fort.

godly/godliness: Being like God in our attitudes and behaviour.

glorify/glorifies: To glorify means to give honour and praise to someone. We should glorify God – we should show that we love him and follow him. Nothing we do or say should bring dishonour to God.

gospel: This is another word for good news. The gospel of Jesus Christ is good news because he has saved his people from their sins. The first four books of the New Testament are specifically called Gospels – The Gospels of Matthew, Mark, Luke and John.

grace and gracious: Grace is the free undeserved blessings and favour that we receive from God. We deserve death and punishment but through Christ's death on the cross God gives all those who believe in him eternal life. This is evidence of his grace.

greaves: Armour that covered the shins.

hamstrung: To break the tendon on the back of the knee, disabling the horse so that it could not run fast.

heaven: This is where those who believe in Christ as their saviour go to when they die. God will take his people there to be with him for all eternity. The souls of believers go to be with the Lord at the moment of their death. On the Day of Judgement their risen, perfect bodies will be reunited with their souls in this glorious, sinless place.

heavenly Hosts: See angels

holy/holiness: To be set apart as different; Faultless; perfect; sinless. God is holy. See 12 Samuel 2: 2 and 1 Peter 1: 16.

house of God/house of the Lord: See Temple/Tabernacle

hyssop: An aromatic plant that is good for cleansing and purification. It was also used in Bible times as a medicine. We read about hyssop at Jesus' crucifixion. (See John 19: 28-30).

idols: An image of a false god. God forbids his people to worship idols in any way. Today we may worship idols such as money, good looks or possessions.

infinite/infinitely: No limits; immeasurable; great or numerous.

iniquity/iniquities: See sin.

javelin: A light spear for throwing.

judgement: When God declares guilt or innocence on a person. With sin comes guilt but with trust in Christ and his sacrifice comes mercy, forgiveness and innocence in the eyes of God the Father.

justice: The quality of being just and fair. Administering the law properly and fairly.

labour in vain: to work for something that is pointless or provides nothing in return.

law: God's law consists of the Ten Commandments and other commands and instructions contained in the Bible in order for us to know how God wants us to live. They were given by God to Moses on Mount Sinai. See Exodus, chapter 20

lutes: Stringed musical instruments.

mortal/immortal: Our lives here will come to an end. Death is a fact of life. Our bodies are mortal; they are not everlasting. With God's gift of faith to his people comes another gift of eternal life and immortality. Our souls that last forever will be reunited with our bodies but these bodies will be transformed, glorious and eternal. Those who trust in Christ will have eternal life. Those who have not trusted in him will be banished to hell forever.

oath: A solemn vow or promise.

offspring: Children.

oracle: A prophesy or statement made by someone who has divine authority.

penitence: See repent; repentance.

perishable/imperishable: Perishable describes things, beings or material that decay. Nothing in this world lasts forever as everything decays. Only the spiritual element of life is imperishable.

praise: This is when we tell God how wonderful he is and how we are thankful for who he is and what he has done for us.

proclaim: To announce.

prophesy/prophesying: When men of God are given messages from the Lord. Prophets in the Bible spoke to people about their sin. They gave warnings from God and told the people what the Lord God had planned for the future.

prophets: Men of God who received direct instructions from God himself to give to the people of God.

prostrated: When someone has fallen on their face. It can be a deliberate action to demonstrate humility.

purification: An act of cleansing, when people would carry out special washing ceremonies required by God before they worshipped him.

refuge: A place of safety.

repent/repentance: This means to turn away from sin to God, showing that you are sorry for your sin and will stop doing it. The desire to repent of sin is given to you by God in his love for you..

resurrection: This is what happened to Jesus when he came back to life on the third day after his crucifixion. If you trust in Jesus you will also be raised to live forever with Jesus in heaven. Those who trust in Jesus will be saved; those who don't will perish.

righteous/righteousness: God is righteous. To be righteous means to be like God – without sin. We can be righteous only because of Jesus. If we turn to him he will cover us with his righteousness. There is nothing in us that is righteous.

sackcloth: Rough material worn by mourners or those in deep distress. They would wear it to show others how they felt.

sacrifice: This is when something is offered up to God as a symbolic gift. In Bible times animals and birds were killed as sacrifices and offered in the temple. Jesus offered himself up as a sacrifice once and for all to cleanse his people from their sin, thus doing away with the need for an more sacrifices for sin.

salvation: This is when Jesus saves his people from their sin. It is what we receive when we repent of our sin and turn back to God. It is deliverance from evil, guilt and pollution of sin through what Jesus has done.

saviour: The name or title given to Jesus because he has saved his people from their sins.

scabbard: A holder for a sword or a dagger.

sceptre: A special ornamental rod which shows that the person holding it has royal authority.

seah: This was a measurement used by the Jews to measure an amount or volume of something.

selah: A Hebrew word which was probably an instruction for the musicians or choir. It may mean pause or stop and listen.

shekel: The money that they used in Israel at that time.

shieldbearer: A man who carried a warrior's shield.

sin: This is any word, act or thought that is against God's law. It includes abstaining from saying, doing or thinking the right thing.

sinners: Those who go against God's Word and disobey him. All humanity are sinners from before birth. It is the very nature of human beings to go against God their Creator. But Christ, who knew no sin, became sin on the cross for those who trust in him, taking their punishment on their behalf.

sinful: To be full of sin.

skins: Animal skins were often used in Bible times to hold liquids such as wine. The pelt would be sewn together into a bag.

sling: A weapon used to throw stones with.

sovereignty: God's absolute power and authority over all creation. Nothing happens without his knowledge. He is in control. He knows what is for the best and even when bad things happen we can trust him. He is all powerful.

staff: A shepherd's stick that was used as a weapon against wild animals as well as something with which to direct the sheep with.

stature: Height.

subject: Bring under the control or authority of another.

subjects: Those who are under the rule of a monarch.

sustain: Support and help.

synagogue: The local place of worship for Jews in Bible times.

tabernacle/temple: This was the place of worship in Jerusalem. People would go there to offer sacrifices to God of young lambs or pigeons. The temple was divided into different areas. One area was called the Most Holy Place where the High Priest went each year to seek forgiveness from God for the sins of the people. During King David's time there was no temple to worship in – what they had was a tabernacle or tent of meeting. God did not allow David to build the Temple. Instead that job was to be left to his son.

temptation: This is something that prompts desire in us to do what is against God's law. Jesus knows what it is like to be tempted. He was tempted by the devil. The difference between

Jesus and us is that we often give into temptation. He never did. Jesus is sinless.

tabernacle: A movable tent-temple which Moses erected for the service of God, made according to the "pattern" which God himself showed to him.

transgress/transgressions/transgressors: See sin/sinners.

tribute: A payment made by one ruler to another.

trustworthy: Faithful.

tunic: This was an item of clothing. In David's case this may have also been a piece of armour or protective clothing to wear in battle.

uncircumscised: God commanded that Hebrew men were circumscised as young babies. This was a physical operation they underwent as a sign of their submission to God. Those nations who were uncircumscised were therefore pagan and in conflict with God.

vindication: If there has been a vindication then someone has been cleared of guilt and suspicion.

worship: This is the act of praising and glorifying God. It is something that God wants us to do. Worship can give us joy but it should be more about giving glory to God than what it gives to us.

worthy: Deserving of something.

wrath: Anger.

wretched: In poor or pitiful circumstances; miserable.

zeal: A great enthusiasm or eagerness.

 MAPS

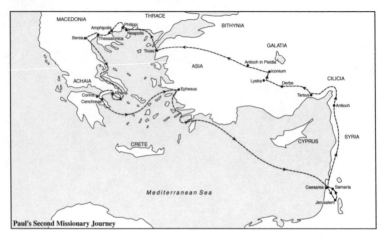

Paul's Second Missionary Journey

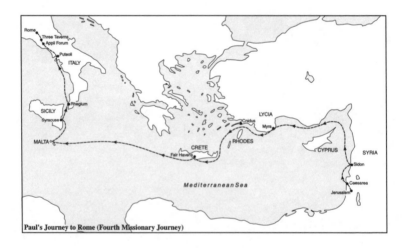

Paul's Journey to Rome (Fourth Missionary Journey)

PLACE NAMES

Arabah: From the Hebrew word meaning plain, or wilderness, Arabah was the term used for the lowland area through which the River Jordan flows south from the Sea of Galilee.

Aram: The name of a region located in central Syria.

Azekah: The name meant 'dug over'. It was situated in the low hills of Judah and guarded the upper reaches of the Valley of Elah. The Amorite kings were defeated here by Joshua and it was given to the tribe of Judah.

Baal Perazim: David defeated the Philistines here. It was a mountain near the Valley of Rephaim and Jerusalem.

Bahurim: A village east of Jerusalem, on the road to the Jordan valley, close to the Mount of Olives.

Bethlehem: Means – house of bread. A town 8 kilometres south of Jerusalem.

Desert of: The term 'desert of' is applied in a general way to the lands about certain places e.g. Maon, Ziph, En Gedi etc.

> **Maon:** In the hills of Judah about 16 kilometres south of Hebron. This was Nabal's home.

> **Ziph:** David hid at Ziph during his flight from Saul. It was south east of Hebron.

Egypt: The land that the Hebrews were enslaved in before they journeyed to the Promised Land.

Ekron: An important Philistine city, south east of Jaffa, near the sea and on the border with Judah. It was the Ark of the Covenant's last resting place before its restoration to Israel.

En Gedi: This was an oasis on the western shore of the Dead Sea. Famous for its vineyards. David hid here from Saul.

Ephes Dammim: A temporary camp of the Philistines when David killed Goliath.

Gath: The royal city of the Philistines on the border with Judah. The birthplace of Goliath and a place of refuge for David during his years as an fugitive. Later David's bodyguard were made up of Gittites i.e. inhabitants of Gath.

Geshur: In the northern part of Bashan, adjoining the kingdom of Aram. In the time of David, Geshur was an independent kingdom. David married a daughter of Talmai, King of Geshur and Absalom was their son. Was also known as Bashan and is today known as the Golan Heights.

Gezer: Located approximately 30 kilometres west of Jerusalem. The view from Gezer encompassed the whole Coastal Plain below it, making it a strategic military centre.

Gibeah: The home town of Saul.

Gibeon: Situated about 8 kilometres north west of Jerusalem.

Gilgal: Saul was made king here.

Giloh: Meaning exile. A city in the southwest part of the hill-country of Judah. It was the residence of Ahithophel 'the Gilonite'.

Hebron: David ruled the Hebrews from Hebron for seven years before moving his capital to Jerusalem. Absalom began his revolt in Hebron.

Hill of Hakilah: David hid here for a while from Saul. It is not far from Jeshimon.

Horesh: Meaning forest. David hid here from Saul. Jonathan Saul's son came to help him and they made a covenant together.

Israel and Judah: You will see that often these two names are mentioned together. The land of Israel at this time was made up of tribal units so if you were an Israelite in Bible times you would identify yourself by your nationality as well as by your tribal name. The tribe of Judah was the tribe that David belonged to. Judah was one of Jacob's sons – and it was through Judah's descendants that God had promised to send a Saviour.

Jerusalem: The Capital city of Israel – near the southern border of the land of Benjamin.

Jeshimon: Found in the wilderness of Judah between the hill country and the Dead Sea. The name means desert.

Jordan: The River Jordan rises in Syria and flows through Lake Tiberias (Sea of Galilee). It drains into the Dead Sea after a course of 360 kilometres. Jesus was baptised here.

Judah: The area allotted to the tribe of Judah

Kidron Valley: This is a valley near Jerusalem and continues east through the Judean Desert towards the Dead Sea.

Lo Debar: Meaning no pasture – this was a town in Gilead not far from Mahanaim, north of the Jabbok.

Metheg Ammah: David conquered the Philistines here. It may have been associated with Gath, but it is not certain where it was or if it was an actual place.

Rabbah: Also referred to as Rabbath. This was the chief city of the Ammonites.

Ramah: Near Gibeon and Mizpah to the West, Gibeah to the South and Geba to the East. About 8 kilometres north of Jerusalem.

Sela Hammahlekoth: Meaning Cliff of Divisions. This is the great gorge which lies between Hachilah and Maon, southeast of Hebron. This was where David and Saul had an interview where each stood on an opposing cliff with the deep chasm in between.

Shaaraim Road: This was a road on the way to Gath and Ekron.

Shiloh: A town that had the tent of meeting in it during the time of the Judges. Where Samuel's mother went to worship the LORD and met with the priest Eli. Situated north of Bethel.

Socoh: Situated in the hill country of Judah south west of Hebron.

Tyre: A town in Phoenicia. Hiram was king of this area.

Valley of Elah: This was the valley in which David slew Goliath. Near Azekah and Socho or Socoh.

Valley of Rephaim: This is a valley descending southwest from Jerusalem to the Valley of Elah below. It is an ancient route from the coastal plain to the Judean Hills.

Well of Sirah: Sirah means thorn. This is the well where Joab and Abishai murdered Abner. Possibly one mile northwest of Hebron.

Zion: A term often used for The Land of Israel and its capital Jerusalem. Can refer to a specific mountain near Jerusalem, Mount Zion on which stood a Jebusite fortress of the same name. This fortress was conquered by David and named the City of David. The term Zion came to mean the area of Jerusalem where the fortress stood and later became a name used to describe the entire city of Jerusalem. It is also used to mean Israel and all its inhabitants, plus God's people of all ages.

BOOT CAMP/001
GETTING STARTED WITH
THE OLD TESTAMENT

GENESIS TO SAMUEL

The Bible is divided into two sections, the Old Testament and the New Testament. The New Testament records what took place in the immediate run up to the birth of Jesus Christ and covers the time of his life on earth and the beginnings of the early church.

The Old Testament is the story of God's people prior to the birth of Christ.

The Old Testament consists of thirty-nine different books and it can also be divided into other sections such as books of history, prophecy, poetry and law.

The first six books of the Old Testament cover the creation of the world up to the arrival of the Hebrew people in the Promised Land. The very first book in the Bible is Genesis. It is called that because this is a book about beginnings. The Word Genesis means beginning. It tells how God made the world and how human beings first sinned against him. Genesis explains what happened as a result of that disobedience. It is in Genesis that we discover why death is now a fact of life. It is because Adam, our representative, disobeyed the creator God. And from that moment on human beings have been siners.

CREATION (GENESIS 1–3).
God created the world and human kind perfectly. There was no sin. The first man and woman, Adam and Eve, lived in the Garden of Eden where there was plenty of food. But there was one tree that God instructed Adam and Eve not to eat from. The devil, in the guise of a serpent, deceived Eve into eating the forbidden fruit. She then gave some to Adam. He ate it too. Sin entered the world. The world was spoiled as was Adam and Eve's relationship with God. God had to banish them from the Garden.

After sin entered the world we read in Genesis of an amazing link to the future. As Adam and Eve, the first examples of humanity, stood in shame before the God they disobeyed a promise was made. Adam and Eve did not make this promise; God did. And God always keeps his promises. He promised that there would be a saviour. In the future a descendant of Adam and Eve would be the one to destroy the power of sin and Satan. And if you've ever read through the Bible and wondered why there are so many genealogies and family trees – well, this is your answer. With a little bit of study into all these names you will soon discover that the people mentioned in Genesis and Exodus, in Joshua, Ruth and 1 Samuel appear again in Matthew chapter 1, in the family tree of Jesus Christ. And you thought all those names were just some very peculiar lists!

Further on in Genesis we are introduced to Abraham. Abraham is the ancestor of many of the Bible characters we read about. Isaac was Abraham's much longed for son and Jacob and Esau were Abraham's grandsons. Jacob went on to have twelve sons of his own – one of whom was Joseph. He was taken against his will to Egypt and eventually his family end up there too. At first the Hebrews lived there in peace and plenty but eventually, Abraham's descendants were enslaved by the Egyptians. That is when Moses and his brother, Aaron, entered onto the scene.

The second book of the Bible is called Exodus because of the Exodus or exit of the Hebrew people from the land of Egypt. God had promised them a land of their own – the land of Canaan. God chose Moses to be the leader of his people and after much struggle the then Pharaoh of Egypt agreed to let the Hebrew people go free. The following four books tell the story of the wilderness wanderings of God's people and their eventual arrival in Canaan; the book of Joshua, the last of the four, recounts the conflicts that took place in order to defeat of the enemy tribes in that land.

God's Word then continues with the books of Judges and Ruth. The events in these books took place at a time when God's people no longer followed God's ways. In fact they were under the influence of the godless nations surrounding them. Each man did in his own eyes what seemed right to himself. Instead of following God's laws and worshipping the one true God the Hebrew people worshipped idols and behaved immorally. A series of judges ruled the land of Israel at that time but that was about to change. God introduced another character to the scene – a prophet – Samuel. And the story of the kings began.

BOOT CAMP/002
GETTING STARTED WITH
DAVID

SAMUEL

Samuel's mother, Hannah, was childless at a time when to be childless was the height of disgrace to a married woman in Israel. Her husband, Elkanah, loved her, but he still had a second wife, Penninah, who made Hannah's life a misery through her malicious teasing. Peninah had no trouble conceiving children and this situation just added to the humiliation and heartache of Hannah.

A family visit to the tabernacle at Shiloh gave Hannah the opportunity to worship God in the tent of meeting. It was there that she poured her heart out to the Lord. She promised him that if he would give her a son she would give him back to the Lord's service.

Eli, the priest, witnessed her grief and after an initial misunderstanding comforted her with a prayer that the Lord would grant her request. Some months later Hannah was the thankful mother of a young son named Samuel. While he was still a young child she returned to Shiloh. She had not forgotten her promise. Samuel was given to Eli the priest as a servant for the tabernacle.

Eli soon realised that this young boy was different. The Lord God spoke to the child. Samuel grew up to be a prophet and one that would stand at a crossroads in the history of the Hebrew people, the people of God.

SAUL

Saul was Israel's first king. His reign began with great promise but failed to live up to that greatness. His pride and arrogance led him away from the one true God. The bashful, slightly awkward young Saul that we meet at first in the book of Samuel ended up as an envious, bitter ruler who visited sorcerers rather than seeking the face of the one true God.

The prophet Samuel was chosen by God to be his spokesperson and was there when the people of God first demanded a king. They had the dubious desire to be like the other nations around them. They thought a human king was the answer. God knew what troubles this would bring but he allowed it to take place. It was after all part of his plan. He saw the future and controled it – and royalty was born.

Saul didn't remain king however. As a result of his disobedience a new king was chosen by God and anointed by Samuel... David. He was a good king, but a flawed human being. It would be the King of kings and Lord of lords who came after him who would be the truly great and perfect king: The Lord Jesus Christ.

Boot camp/003
Getting Started With You

WHO ARE YOU?

When asked that question you'll give your name. You might add something about where you are from and what you do. Someone else has different answers. There is nobody else exactly like you. However, there are things that everybody has in common.

1. We are all human beings. God created us.

CREATED BY GOD
This means made by God. God is our Creator. He made the world. The universe and everything that exists in it is his creation.

SOUL
God breathed into Adam (the first man) the breath of life and Adam became a living soul. You have a soul too; you aren't just a body. Your soul will last forever, either in heaven or in hell. Our bodies will also last forever after they are resurrected. God tells us in his Word that we are to love the Lord our God with all our heart, soul and mind (Matthew 22: 37).

2. We all sin. We disobey God.

SIN
This is disobedience to God's instructions in thoughts, words or deeds. Sin is failing to match the perfect standard God has set. If we do not listen to or obey God then we don't love him. That is sin. The devil tempts us to sin. Our own sinful nature tempts us too. We can so easily sin even when we don't want to.

TEMPTATION
God has promised to deliver us from temptation if we ask him. He won't allow us to be tempted beyond what we can endure.

3. Sin deserves God's punishment but God rescues us through Christ's death on the cross.

PUNISHMENT
The punishment for sin is eternal death in hell. So sin is a big problem for all of us. You may think that you aren't that bad. But

135

we cannot get to heaven on our own. God's Word tells us that if we trust in Jesus Christ we will be given eternal life. Remember that 'the wages of sin is death but the gift of God is eternal life through Jesus Christ his Son.'

HELL
Those who do not turn away from sin to follow Christ go to hell when they die. Just as heaven is for ever so is hell. It is an eternal death instead of an eternal life.

THE DEVIL
He is in conflict with God. He tempted the first human beings. Sin, death and the devil have been defeated by Jesus Christ and his death on the cross.

4. But the gift of God is eternal life through Jesus Christ his Son.

ETERNAL LIFE
Eternal life starts the moment you trust in Jesus, but it means that death is not the end and that life, abundant life, continues in heaven for ever after.

HEAVEN
This is one of the places that you can go to when you die. You can only go there if you love and trust in Jesus Christ. Heaven is perfect in every way because it is where God is. There is no sin there. It is the place where those who believe in Jesus Christ will live for ever.

Does the fact that God is willing to give you a gift make you wonder about what God is like? Lets find out!

BOOT CAMP/004
GETTING STARTED WITH GOD

WHO IS GOD AND WHAT IS HE LIKE?

Have you ever tried to describe someone when they are not there? You might describe their appearance, their likes and dislikes, how they behave, what they do. But a verbal description doesn't really show what your friend is like? To know what someone is really like you have to meet them for yourself.

Describing what God is like is difficult too. You can't see God because he is a Spirit, he doesn't have a body. Jesus Christ, also known as God the Son, does have a body. Jesus was on earth for a while, but is now in heaven. We can't physically see God the Father. We can't see God the Son either – at least not yet. So how can we know God for ourselves? What is he like? The Bible tells us some things:
1. God is faithful: Deuteronomy 7: 9.
2. God is love: Romans 5: 8.
3. God is just or fair: Psalm 9: 16.

There are many other things that we can find out about God in his Word, the Bible.

HOW SHOULD WE FEEL TOWARDS GOD?

The Bible often mentions that people are supposed to fear God. This is not the same fear that we feel when we are scared of the dark or of heights. When the Bible refers to the words 'fear of God' it means that God's people are in awe of their Creator, they show deep respect to him. They realise that he is all powerful but also loving and merciful. They depend on him for their very existence and they also need him, and only him, for their eternal security.

We are supposed to trust in him and love him. But our faith and love towards God is actually something that we need to receive from God in the first place. (See Ephesians 2: 8 and 1 John 4: 19). Faith in God, belief in him is something you should ask God for.

GOD'S WORD; THE BIBLE

It was written by different people but each of them was told by God what to write by God. So God is the author of this book, the Bible. He inspired it. The writers who wrote the Old and New Testaments wrote these words under Divine inspiration.

137

DOES GOD HAVE A NAME?

Throughout the Bible there are many different names for God. Each has its own meaning. They tell us something about God's character and who he is. Some of these names are directly attributed to the Son of God – Jesus Christ. Particularly those names mentioned in Revelation: Faithful and True; King of kings and Lord of lords.

God's names tell us about his power: The LORD Almighty; The LORD God Almighty; The LORD strong and Mighty; Mighty God; Rock of Israel; The Rock my Saviour.

God's names tell us about his position and authority: The Most High; The God of the armies of Israel; The One enthroned in Heaven; King of glory; King of kings and Lord of lords; Prince of Peace.

God's names tell us about his nature:
He is alive: The Living God.
He is sinless and holy: The Holy One.
He is trustworthy: Faithful and True.
He is eternal: Everlasting Father.

God's names teach us about the history of God's people: The God of Jacob; The God of Israel; The God of the armies of Israel. Through these names we are also reminded of all the promises that God has made to particular individuals in the Bible – and we know that he has kept these promises.

God's names teach us about the Trinity: The Spirit of the Lord, the Everlasting Father and the Son.

God's names teach us about what God does:
He rules: The one enthroned in heaven; King of kings and Lord of lords; Prince of peace.
He cares: Shepherd and Overseer of your soul.
He saves: Saviour; Christ; the Rock my Saviour.
He teaches: Wonderful Counsellor.

Jesus Christ, the second person of the Godhead or Trinity has names that are particular to him.

Jesus Son of David: This name shows us that Jesus is in the royal ancestral line of David. The fact that he is in David's family tree is one thing that proves he is the promised Messiah.

Messiah (Christ): comes from a Hebrew word which means the Anointed (One), someone anointed with holy anointing oil, and having been chosen for a task; this gives Messiah the additional meaning of Chosen (One), especially divinely chosen. The word Christ is the Greek version of Messiah.

The Trinity: is a term use to describe the three persons of the Godhead. God the Father, God the Son and God the Holy Spirit are three persons in one God – all one in purpose and equal in power and glory.

God the Father: is the first person of the Trinity. Jesus Christ speaks and acts on behalf of his people before God the Father. He prayed to God the Father often when he was on earth, especially for those whom God the Father had given to him to be his people.

God the Son: is the second person of the Trinity. God the Father loved sinners so much that he sent God the Son, whom we know as the Lord Jesus Christ, so that anyone who would believe in him would not perish but would have eternal life.

God the Holy Spirit: is the third person in the Trinity. Jesus had promised his followers that though he had to leave this world and return to God the Father in heaven, he would send them another comforter who would never leave his people. And he did. God the Holy Spirit was sent in a special and dramatic way soon after Jesus Christ ascended to heaven and he has remained with God's people throughout the years.

Through the names of God we learn about our relationship to him: the LORD your God; the Rock my Saviour; Father.

Is this your God? Is he your Rock, your Saviour and is God your Father? Do you love him and trust in him? He is the one and only true God and is worthy of your trust and your worship. God our heavenly Father is everything that a Father should be. Earthly fathers fail us but God never fails us.

Have you turned from your sin and asked God to forgive your sins through his Son Jesus Christ? If you have then the LORD is your God and Christ is your Rock and your Saviour. If you haven't trusted in Christ for the forgiveness of your sins then you are lost and will perish without him. All other gods are false. Giving your life to something or someone other than the one true God is a waste, a vain hope. There is no salvation unless you turn to the one true Saviour.

BOOT CAMP/005
GETTING STARTED WITH
JESUS CHRIST

WHO IS JESUS CHRIST AND HOW CAN I KNOW HIM?

To really know someone you have to get to know them personally. It is the same with God. The only way we can really get to know God is through Jesus Christ, his Son. Jesus came to earth to bring people back to God.

1. Jesus Christ came to earth as a baby, born of a virgin by the power of the Holy Spirit.

Jesus was born as a human baby. He was fully man and fully God. His birth fulfilled many Old Testament prophecies: he was born of a virgin; he was born in Bethlehem; a descendant of David; from the tribe of Judah.

CHRISTMAS
Read the REAL Christmas story for yourself in Matthew chapters 1 and 2; and Luke chapters 1-2.

2. Jesus Christ is God and Man; Divine and Human.

Because he was God he was sinless and because he was God and man he was the only one who could take God's punishment for humanity's sin. This is what happened when he died on the cross. Jesus took this punishment from God his Father so that we can be saved from sin. When you trust in Jesus Christ, when you believe that he has taken the punishment for your sin, when you turn from your sin and give your love to God – you will be saved.

DIVINE AUTHORITY
Jesus Christ has all power and authority. This has been given to him by God the Father. He has authority over creation, sickness and disease. He even has authority over death and sin. He can forgive sins. He conquered sin, death and the devil on the cross. His authority and control is over all things. The devil can do nothing that is outside God's control. God has authority over you and me.

There is nothing that can separate us from his love when we trust in him. There are no leaders or powers that can thwart his plans or purposes.

CRUCIFIXION
This was the method of execution that the Romans used at the time of the occupation of Palestine. It is the method they used to kill Jesus. A cross was made out of wood, onto which a criminal was nailed. The criminal was then left to hang there until he died. The Jewish religious leaders falsely accused Jesus of many things and then handed him over to the Roman authorities. Pilate, the Roman governor, made a weak attempt to free Jesus but in the end he agreed to crucify him.

Note that there is more to Christ's crucifixion than a murder. Jesus had to die in order to save people from their sins. The punishment for sin had to be paid otherwise sinners would not be allowed into heaven. So although this crucifixion is a dreadful event, it is also the one event that brings sinners back to God.

RESURRECTION
The resurrection is what happened three days after the death of Jesus Christ. He was raised to life again. This shows that he had accomplished everything he had come to do. He had defeated the power of sin and death. His body was raised from the dead. All who trust in Christ will be raised to life again too, with bodies that will last forever. With these bodies we will be with Jesus for all eternity – sinless, holy and praising God.

ASCENSION
After the resurrection Jesus was seen by many people. After he had promised the disciples the gift of the Holy Spirit, Jesus ascended to heaven in a cloud. Right now he is in the presence of God the Father and he is praying for his people.

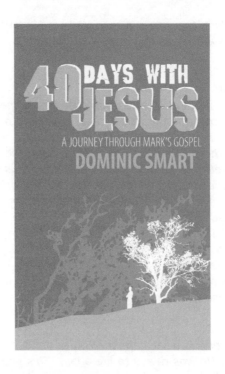

YOUR MISSION SHOULD YOU CHOOSE TO ACCEPT IT IS TO READ THROUGH THE GOSPEL OF MARK IN 40 DAYS!

You can investigate one of the most fascinating people this world has ever known: Jesus Christ, the Son of God. Go on this journey with someone who lived at the same time and who was a friend of Jesus' disciples – Mark.

Beginners will find the usual helps and extra features to assist them. Boot Camps; Maps and Extra Information is provided throughout the book.

Dominic Smart is the minister of Gilcomston Parish Church, Aberdeen, Scotland.

ISBN: 978-1-84550-193-8

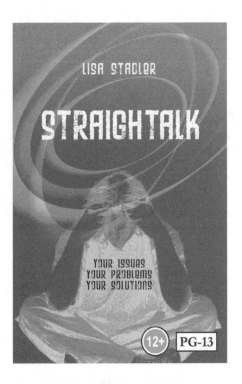

PROBLEMS! LIKE I DON'T HAVE ENOUGH OF THEM ALREADY!

If that's you saying those words then this book could be just what you are looking for. If you've just been dumped, your teachers are onto you about cutting class and things are going from bad to worse; God can help you deal with your problems and the problems of others. His strength will give you courage to do what is right. Give your heartache to God and live life to the full.

Each chapter of Straightalk details a teen-specific life or family issue with real-life discussion and prayer. Scripture verses give God's direct input to your problems.

Lisa Stadler uses the commonsense and wisdom that God has given her through his Word. Lisa wants young people to discover God's answers. She has a Masters degree in Biblical Studies and is now working on a PhD in Psychology.

ISBN: 978-1-84550-260-7